Anthems Old & New

100 settings for parish choirs
selected by Christopher Tambling

VOLUME TWO

Kevin Mayhew

We hope you enjoy the music in this book. Further copies are available
from your local music shop or Christian bookshop.

In case of difficulty, please contact the publisher direct by writing to:

The Sales Department
KEVIN MAYHEW LTD
Buxhall
Stowmarket
Suffolk
IP14 3BW

Phone 01449 737978
Fax 01449 737834
E-mail info@kevinmayhewltd.com

Please ask for our complete catalogue of outstanding Church Music.

First published in Great Britain in 2000 by Kevin Mayhew Ltd.

ISBN 1 84003 573 0
ISMN M 57004 710 9
Catalogue No: 1450181

0 1 2 3 4 5 6 7 8 9

Front Cover: The North Transept window, St Albans Cathedral.
Photograph by Derek Forss. Reproduced by kind permission.
Cover design by Jaquetta Sergeant.

Music selected by Christopher Tambling
Music setting by Donald Thomson

Printed by Colorcraft Hong Kong

Contents

Index of Uses

ALL PEOPLE THAT ON EARTH DO DWELL

The Old Hundredth Psalm Tune

Text: William Kethe, from 'Day's Psalter' (1560-1561)
Music: Ralph Vaughan Williams (1872-1958)
Faux-bourdon by John Dowland (1562-1626)

* The congregation may sing in vs. 1, 2 and 5.

* Cue-sized notes for Organ

ways, for it is seem - ly so to do.

4. For why? the Lord our God is good. His mer - cy is for

e - ver sure; his truth at all times firm - ly

to age en - dure.

stood, and shall from age to age en - dure.

* Original text: 'from men and from the angel-host'

Bb TRUMPET DESCANT FOR VERSE 3

ALMIGHTY GOD, WHICH HAST ME BROUGHT

Text: William Leighton (c.1565-1622)
Music: Thomas Ford (1580-1648) arr. Harrison Oxley (b.1933)

AN UPPER ROOM

Text: Fred Pratt Green (b.1903)
Music: John Marsh (b.1939)
based on the Somerset folk song 'O waly waly'

feet, for ser-vice, too, is sa-cra - ment. In him our

joy shall be made com - plete, sent out to serve, as he was

sent. No end there is: we de-part in

peace. He loves be - yond our ut - ter - most: in ev - 'ry
room in our Fa - ther's house he will be
there, as Lord and host.

ANGEL-VOICES EVER SINGING

Text: Francis Pott (1830-1909)
Music: Christopher Tambling (b.1964) based on the melody 'Angel Voices'
by Edwin George Monk (1819-1900)

man? Can we know that thou art near us, and wilt hear us?

Yes, we can.

Sopranos and Altos

For we know that thou re - joic - est o'er each work of

Man.

thine; thou did'st ears and hands and voi-ces for thy praise de-

Tenors and Basses

sign; crafts-man's art and mu-sic's mea-sure for thy plea-sure

Ped.

all com - bine.

dim.

In thy house, great God, we of-fer of thine own to

Organ ad lib.

Anthems

ASCENSION CAROL

Text: Harrison Oxley (b.1933)
Music: 17th Century Dutch song arr. Charles Wood (1866-1926)
Descant by Harrison Oxley (b.1933)

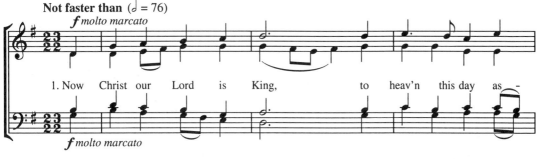

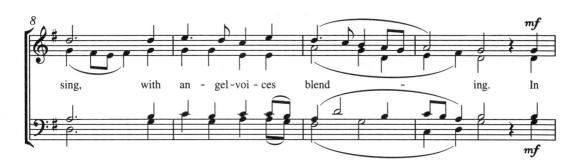

joy to tune our strain with all our might en - dea -

vour. This part - ing brings no pain! For Christ is ours for

e - ver, for e - ver, for e - ver, for

Optional Descant

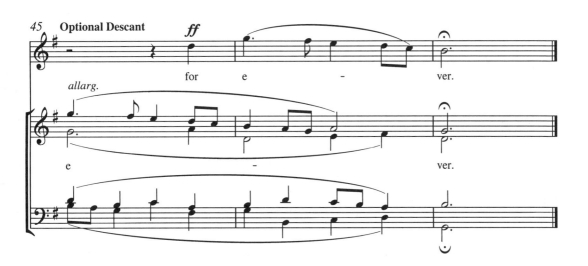

for e - ver.

e - ver.

AVE MARIA

Text: Luke 1
Music: Giulio Caccini (c.1545-1618) arr. Christopher Tambling

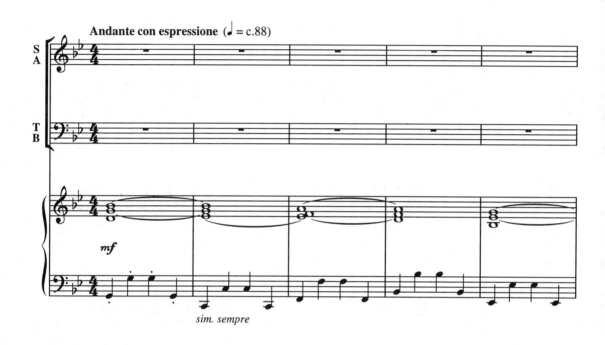

ve.

AVE MARIA

Latin Text: from Luke 1
English Text: Neil Jenkins
Music: adapted from J.S. Bach by Charles Gounod (1818-1893)
arr. Colin Mawby (b.1936)

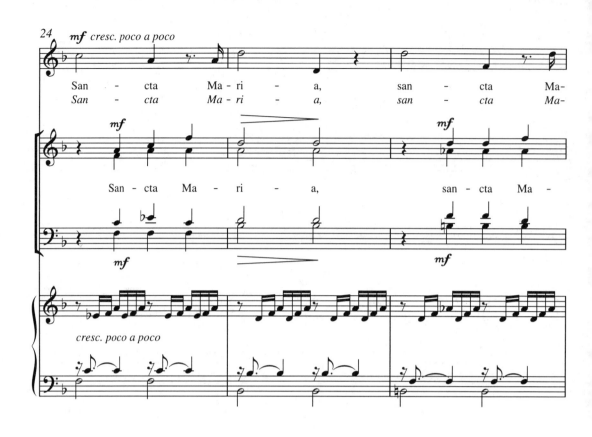

mor – tis no – strae. A – men.
world with - out end. A - men.

A –

A - - men.
A - - men.
- - men.

AVE MARIS STELLA

Text: 9th Century trans. unknown
Music: Richard Shephard (b.1949)

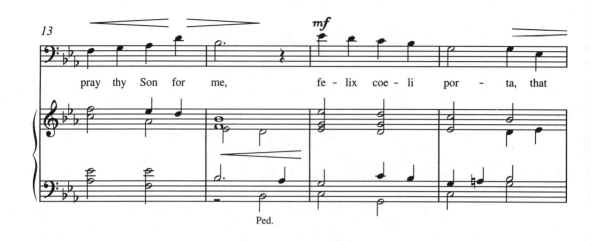

pray thy Son for me, fe - lix coe - li por - ta, that

Ga - bri - el that arch - an - gel,

I may come to thee Ga - bri -

el was mes - sen - ger,

so fair he gree - ted our La - dy

he was mes - sen - ger, so fair he gree - ted Ma - ry

so fair he gree - ted Ma - ry

el was mes - sen - ger, so fair he gree - ted Ma - ry

with A - ve so clear.

Sopranos

Bles - sed be thou Ma - ry, mo - ther so mild,

bles - sed be thou, and Je - sus thy child.

AVE VERUM CORPUS

Text: 14th century attributed to Pope Innocent VI (d.1342)
Music: William Byrd (1543-1623)

See page 58 for a translation of the text.

AVE VERUM CORPUS

Text: 14th century attributed to Pope Innocent VI (d.1342)
Music: Colin Mawby (b.1936)

See page 58 for a translation of the text.

flu - xit a - qua: e - sto no - bis prae - gu -

flu - xit a - qua: e - sto no - bis prae - gu -

san - gui - ne: e - sto no - bis, no - bis,

san - gui - ne: e - sto no - bis,

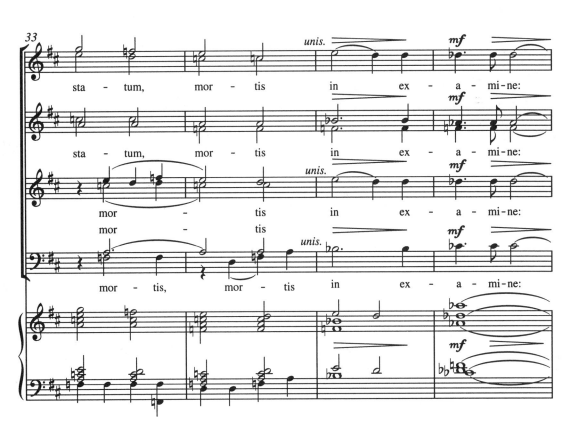

sta - tum, mor - tis in ex - a - mi - ne:

sta - tum, mor - tis in ex - a - mi - ne:

mor - tis in ex - a - mi - ne:

mor - tis, mor - tis in ex - a - mi - ne:

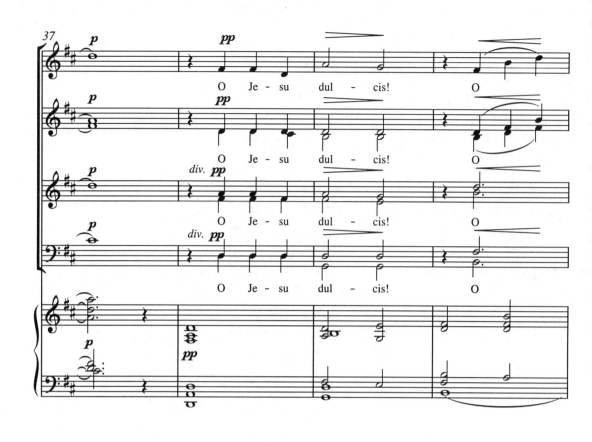

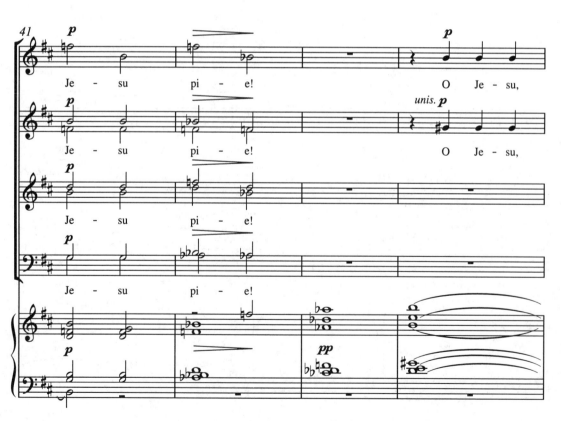

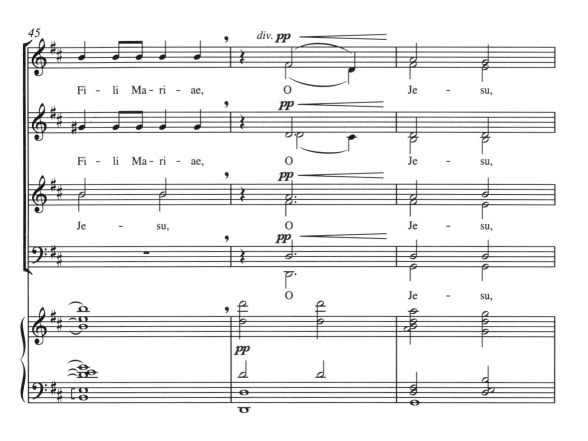

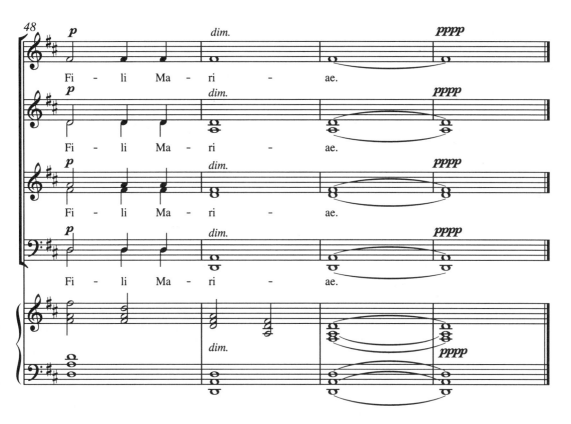

AVE VERUM CORPUS

Text: 14th century attributed to Pope Innocent VI (d.1342)
Music: Wolfgang Amadeus Mozart (1756-1791)

Translation: Hail, true body born of the Virgin Mary which truly suffered and was sacrificed on the cross for the human race, whose pierced side poured with water and blood: be to us a foretaste of the verdict to be passed at death.

im – mo – la – tum in cru – ce pro

im – mo – la – tum in cru – ce pro

im – mo – la – tum in cru – ce pro

im – mo – la – tum in cru – ce pro

ho – mi – ne.

ho – mi – ne.

ho – mi – ne.

ho – mi – ne.

dim.

AVE VIRGO SANCTISSIMA

Text: from a motet by Guerrero
Music: from 'The Last Spring' Edvard Grieg (1843-1907)
arr. Christopher Tambling

Anthems

CALL TO REMEMBRANCE

Text: Psalm 25:5-6
Music: Richard Farrant (d.1580) arr. Harrison Oxley (b.1933)

not the sins and of - fen - ces of my youth: but ac -

not the sins and of - fen - ces of my youth: but ac - cord - ing

not the sins and of - fen - ces of my youth: but ac - cord - ing

not the sins and of - fen - ces of my youth: but ac - cord - ing

cord - ing to thy mer - cy think thou on me, O

to thy mer - cy think thou on me, O

to thy mer - cy think thou on me, O

to thy mer - cy think thou on me, O

CANTATE DOMINO

Text: Psalm 149:1-2; English text by Harrison Oxley (b.1933)
Music: Giuseppe Ottavio Pitoni (1657-1743) arr. Harrison Oxley

COME, HOLY GHOST

Text: John Cosin (1594-1672) based on 'Veni, Creator Spiritus'
Music: Thomas Attwood (1765-1838)

soil - ed face, with the a - bun - dance of thy grace.

Keep far our foes, give peace at home, where thou art guide, no

ill can come; where thou art guide, no ill can come.

Teach us to know the

Fa - ther, Son, and thee of both to be but one, that

through the a - ges all a - long, this may be our end - less song: praise to thy e - ter - nal me - rit, Fa - ther, Son, and Ho - ly Spi - rit, Fa - ther, Son, and Ho - ly Spi - rit.

COME, SPIRIT OF OUR GOD

Text: Michael Forster (b.1946)
Music: Alan Rees (b.1946)

COMFORT, O LORD, THE SOUL OF THY SERVANT

Text: Psalm 26
Music: William Crotch (1775-1847)
from the anthem 'Be merciful unto me'

Com- fort, O Lord, the soul of thy ser - vant, for un - to

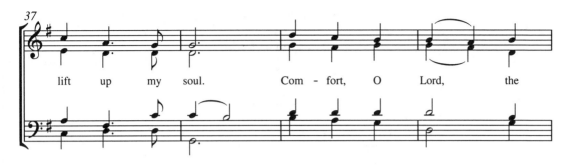

lift up my soul. Com - fort, O Lord, the

soul of thy ser - vant, for un - to thee do I lift up my

soul, do I lift up my soul.

For Malcolm Archer and the Choir of Bristol Cathedral.

EASTERN MONARCHS, SAGES THREE

Text: 15th Century Latin from Leisentrit's 'Gesangbuch' (1567)
Music: Herbert Sumsion (1899-1995)

1. Eas - tern mon - archs, Sa - ges three, come with gifts in great plen - ty, wor - ship Christ on bend - ed knee cum Vir - gi - ne Ma - ri - a.

2. Gold, in hon - our of the King, in - cense to the Priest they bring, myrrh, for time of bu - ry - ing cum Vir - gi - ne Ma - ri - a.

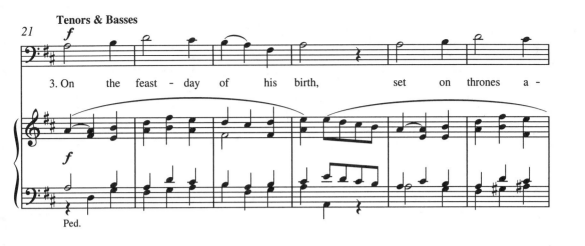

Tenors & Basses

3. On the feast - day of his birth, set on thrones a -

Ped.

bove the earth, an - gels chant in ho - ly

mirth cum Vir - gi - ne Ma - ri - a.

EVENING HYMN

Text: John Keble (1792-1866)
Music: June Nixon based on the melody 'Abends'
by Herbert Stanley Oakeley (1830-1903)

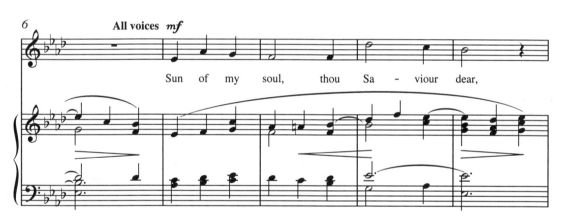

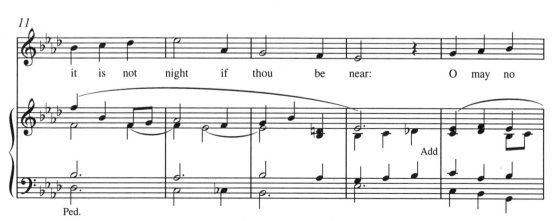

Sections within square brackets are for rehearsal only.

for with - out thee I can - not live; a - bide with

for with - out thee I can - not live; a - bide with

for with - out thee I can - not live; a - bide with

for with - out thee I can - not live; a - bide with

me when night is nigh, for with - out thee I

me when night is nigh, for with - out thee I

me when night is nigh, for with - out thee I

me when night is nigh, for with - out thee I

world our way we take; till in the o - cean of thy

world our way we take; till in the o - cean of thy

Full Sw.

cresc.

love we lose our - selves in heav'n a - bove.

love we lose our - selves in heav'n a - bove.

Add

Anthems

FINISHED THE STRIFE OF BATTLE NOW

Text: trans. John Mason Neale (1816-1866)
Music: Andrew Moore (b.1954) based on the melody 'Surrexit'
by Gregory Murray (1905-1992)

On Eas-ter morn-ing he a-rose, shin-ing with vic-t'ry o'er his foes;

earth is sing-ing, heav'n is ring-ing: al-le-lu-ia, al-le-lu-

ia!

Tenors & Basses *mf*

Clo-sed hath he hell's

poco dim.

Solo

FORTY DAYS AND FORTY NIGHTS

Text: George Hunt Smyttan (1822-1870) and Francis Pott (1832-1909)
Music: Harrison Oxley (b.1936) based on the melody 'Aus der Tiefe'
from the 'Nürnbergisches Gesangbuch' (1676)

dim.

thou, his van-qui-sher be-fore, grant we may not

dim.

41

faint nor fail.

mf

p Sw. or Ch.

Man.

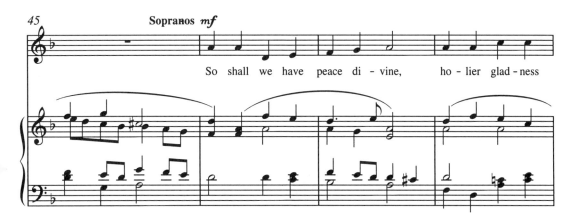

45

Sopranos *mf*

So shall we have peace di-vine, ho-lier glad-ness

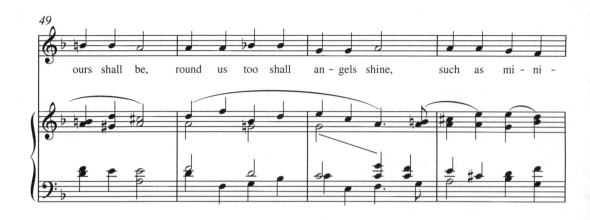

ours shall be, round us too shall an - gels shine, such as mi - ni -

stered to thee.

Keep, O keep us, Sa - viour dear,

Keep, O keep us, Sa - viour dear,

FROM ALL THAT DWELL BELOW THE SKIES

Text: Isaac Watts (1674-1748)
Music: Thomas Attwood Walmisley (1814-1856)

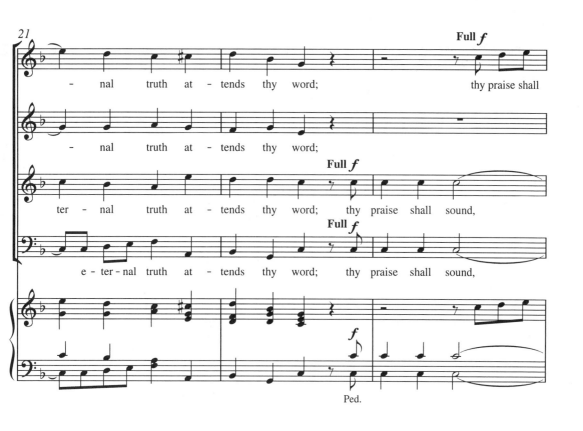

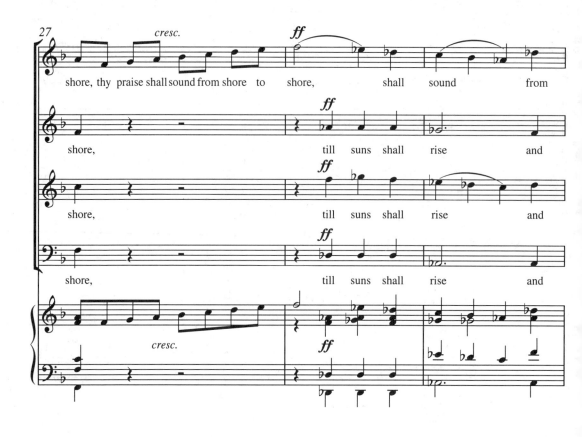

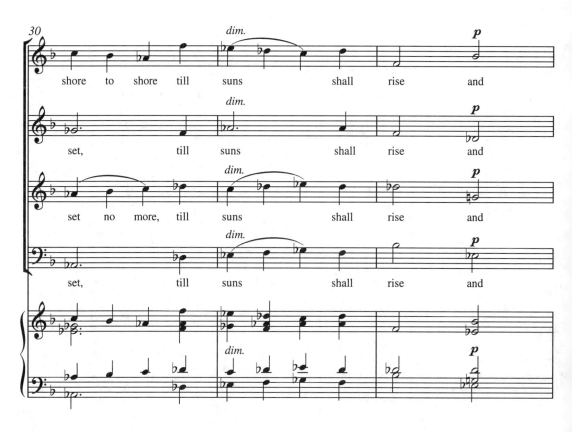

GLORY TO GOD IN THE HIGHEST

Text: translated from the German by Christopher Tambling (b.1964)
Music: Franz Schubert (1797-1828) from the 'German Mass'

* A cappella ad lib.

Anthems

GOD BE IN MY HEAD

Text: Sarum Primer (1558)

Music: Henry Walford Davies (1869-1941) arr. Harrison Oxley (b.1933)

GOD IS ASCENDED

Text: trans. Henry More (1614-1687) and George Ratcliffe Woodward (1848-1934)
Music: 16th century German melody arr. Richard Lloyd (b.1933)

ia,   al - le - lu - ia.   Sov - ran of   sky, and sea, and land,
With De - o   gra - ci - as   al - ways,

al - le - lu - ia,   al - le - lu - ia,   al - le - lu - ia.

5. God is as - cen - ded up on high,   al - le - lu - ia,

al - le - lu - ia.   With mer - ry noise of trum - pet's sound,   al - le - lu -

ia,   al - le - lu - ia,   al - le - lu - ia,   al - le - lu - ia!

Anthems

GOD IS WHY I AM

Text: Brian Foley (b.1919)
Music: June Nixon

why of all I am, and all I am to be.

why of all I am, and all I am to be.

why of all I am, all I am to be.

why of all I am, and all I am to be.

mf

Ped.   Man.

mf   *cresc.*

If this it-self is praise to you, your bring-ing me to be, you

mf   *cresc.*

If this it-self is praise, your bring-ing me to be, you

mf   *cresc.*

If this it-self is praise, your bring-ing me to be, you

mf   *cresc.*

This it-self is praise, your bring-ing me to be, you

all you gave to me, find worth, find praise of you in all I

you gave to me, find praise of you my God in all I

all you gave to me, find praise of you my God in all I

worth, find praise of you, find praise of you my God in all I

come to be.

come to be.

come to be.

come to be.

GOD OMNIPOTENT REIGNETH

Text: George Ratcliffe Woodward (1884-1934) from Psalm 93
Music: Pierre Daques (16th century) set by Charles Wood (1866-1929)
arr. Harrison Oxley (b.1933)

might; by him the world a - lone im - mu - ta - bly was ground - ed; in heav'n hath he his throne, from e - ver - last - ing foun - ded.

Ped.

Reduce
Man.

All voices
f sempre marcato

O - cean bil - low and break - er up - lift the

voice of pride; but their migh - ti - er

mak - er go - ver-neth wind and tide.

GOD SO LOVED THE WORLD

Text: John 3:16
Music: John Stainer (1840-1901)

Anthems

HALLELUJAH CHORUS from 'MESSIAH'

Text: from Scripture
Music: George Frideric Handel (1685-1759) arr. Colin Hand

hal-le - lu-jah, hal-le - lu-jah, hal-le - lu-jah, hal-le - lu-jah,

reign - eth, hal-le - lu-jah, hal-le - lu - jah, hal-le - lu-jah, hal-le - lu-jah,

reign - eth, hal-le - lu-jah, hal-le - lu - jah, hal-le - lu-jah, hal-le - lu-jah,

reign - eth, hal-le - lu-jah, hal-le - lu-jah, hal-le - lu-jah, hal-le - lu-jah,

Reeds

Reeds off

Man.

for   the   Lord   God om - ni -   po - tent

hal-le-

hal - le - lu - jah,   hal - le - lu - jah,   hal - le - lu - jah,   hal -

Where the text '-jah, hal-' is to be sung to one note, the two syllables should be run together.

reign for e - ver, for e - ver and e - ver, King of

he shall reign for e - ver and e - ver, King of

reign for e - ver, for e - ver and e - ver, King of

reign for e - ver, for e - ver and e - ver, King of

L.H. Reed

kings, and Lord of lords, King of kings, and Lord of

kings, and Lord of lords, King of kings, and Lord of

kings, and Lord of lords, King of kings, and Lord of

kings, and Lord of lords, King of kings, and Lord of

HARK, WHAT A SOUND

Text: Frederick Myers (1843-1903)
Music: Andrew Fletcher (b.1950) based on the melody 'Highwood'
by Richard Runciman Terry (1865-1938)

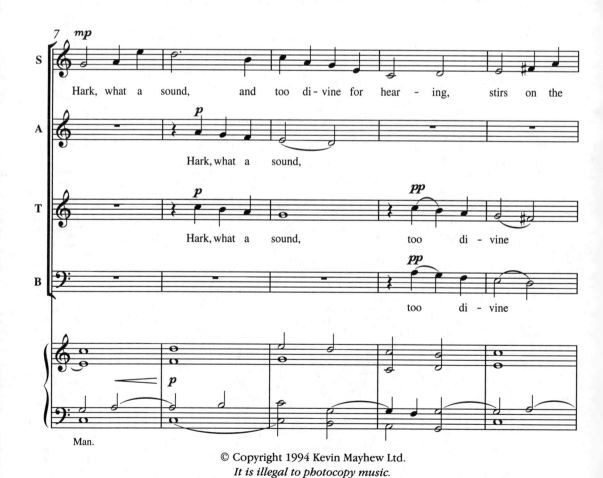

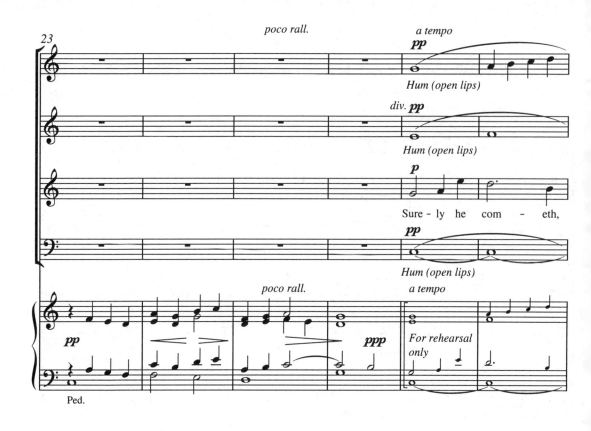

HERE, O MY LORD

Text: Horatius Bonar (1808-1889)
Music: Alan Viner (b.1951)

Anthems

HOLY, HOLY, HOLY

Text: Reginald Heber (1783-1826)
Music: Peter Ilyich Tchaikovsky (1840-1893) arr. Harrison Oxley (b.1933)

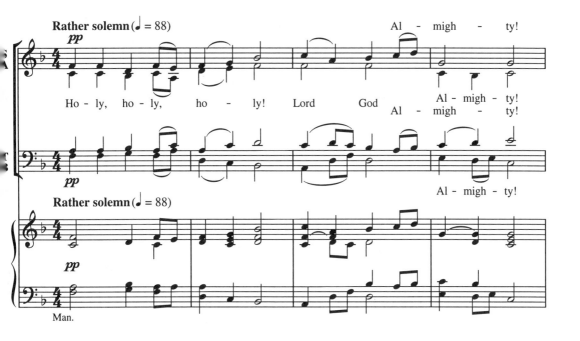

per - fect in pow - er, in love, and pu - ri - ty.

Più vivo (♩ = 100)

Ho - ly, ho - ly, ho - ly! Lord God al - migh - ty! All thy works shall praise thy name in

HOSANNA TO THE SON OF DAVID

Text: from the Palm Sunday Liturgy (Sarum Rite)
Music: Herbert Sumsion (1899-1995)

san - na!   Ho - san - na!   Ho - san - na!

Tempo moderato

Be - hold, your King comes to you, O Zi - on,

meek and low - ly,   sit - ting u - pon an ass.

scep - tre of your king - dom as a right - eous scep - tre.

You have loved right-eous-ness and ha - ted e - vil; there-fore

God, your God, has a - noint-ed you with the oil of

HOW BEAUTEOUS ARE THEIR FEET

Text: Isaac Watts (1674-1748)
Music: Charles Villiers Stanford (1852-1924) arr. Harrison Oxley (b.1933)

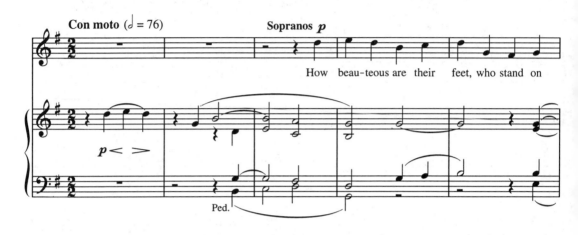

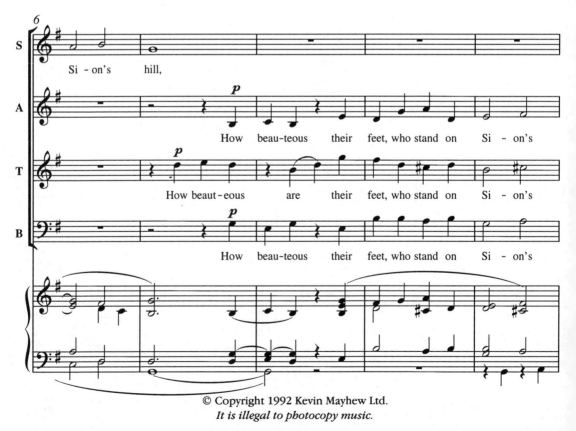

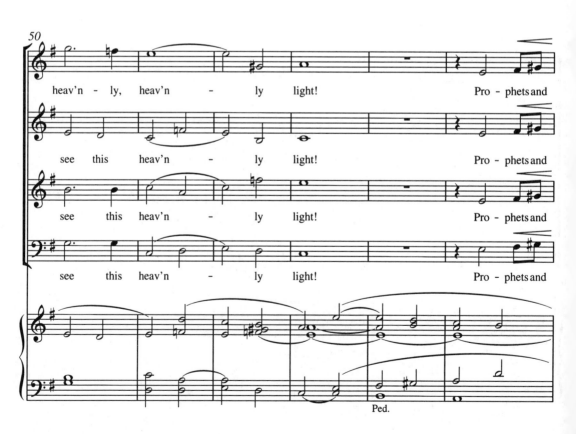

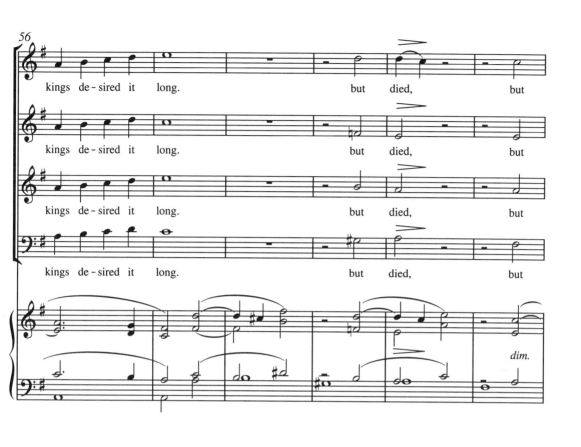

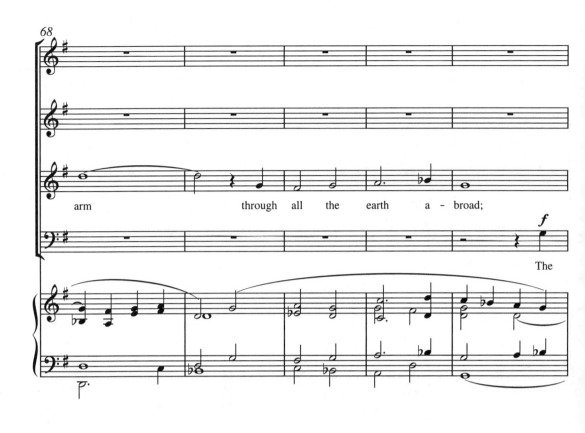

arm ... through all the earth a - broad;

f

The

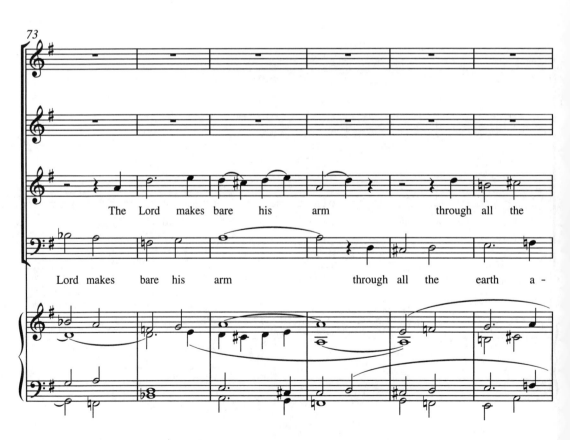

The Lord makes bare his arm through all the

Lord makes bare his arm through all the earth a -

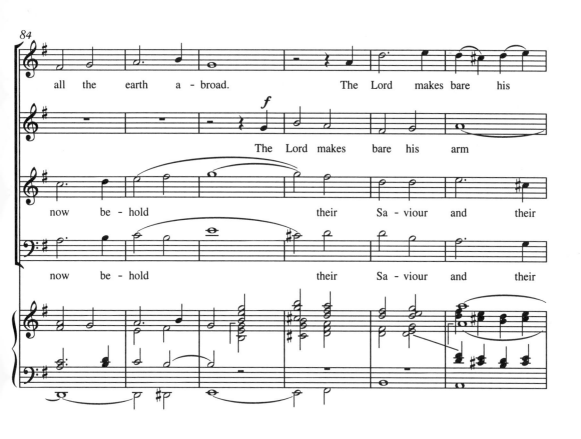

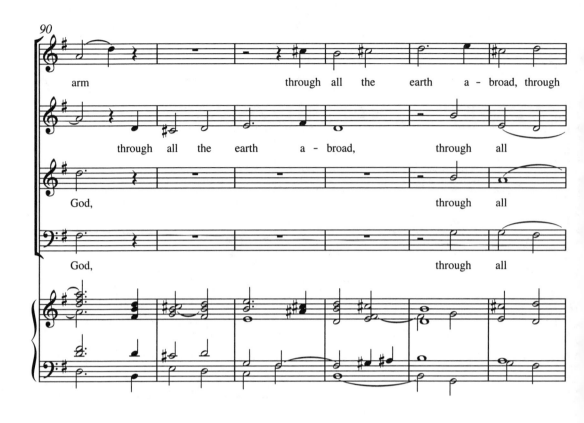

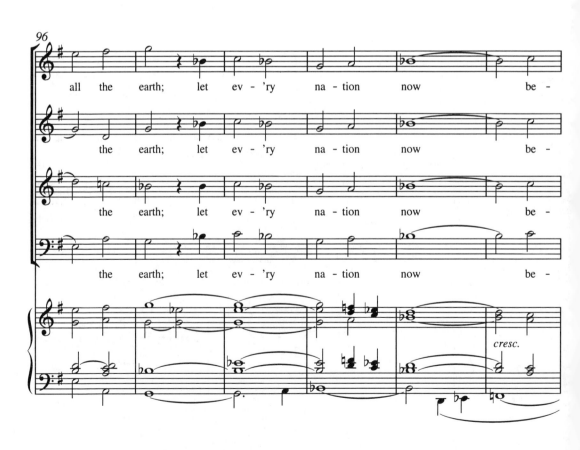

HYMN OF ST PATRICK

Text: from 'The Hymn of St Patrick' trans. Cecil Frances Alexander (1818-1895)
Music: Margaret Rizza (b.1929)

I AM THE VINE

Text: Margaret Bowdler (b.1939)
Music: Norman Warren (b.1934)

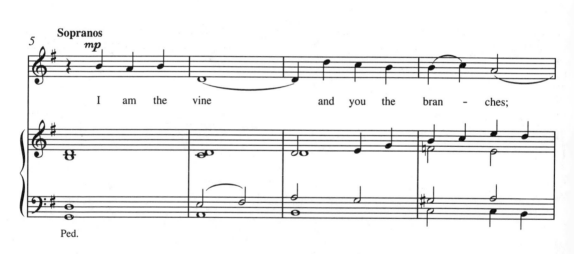

bear much fruit.

I am the vine and you the bran - ches;

if you a - bide in me your lives will

I will come to you, and I will come to you to make your heart my home.

Rest in my love, and let it flow through you

Rest in my love, and let it

Man.

I WAITED FOR THE LORD from 'HYMN OF PRAISE'

Text: Psalm 40: 1, 5
Music: Felix Mendelssohn (1809-1847) arr. Harrison Oxley

* Originally ♪ = 100

plaint. I wai – ted for the Lord, he in – cli – ned un – to

me; he heard my com-plaint, he heard my com-

plaint. O blest are they that hope and trust in the

Lord! O blest are they that hope and trust in the Lord! I

O blest are they that hope and trust in the Lord!

O blest are they that hope and trust in the Lord!

O blest are they that hope and trust in the Lord!

I wai - ted for the Lord, he in - cli - ned un -

wai - ted for the Lord, he in - cli - ned un - to me; he

I WILL LIFT UP MINE EYES

Text: from Psalm 121
Music: Alan Ridout (1934-1996)

keep - er,   the Lord is thy de - fence   u -

pon thy right   hand.   The Lord shall pre - serve   thy

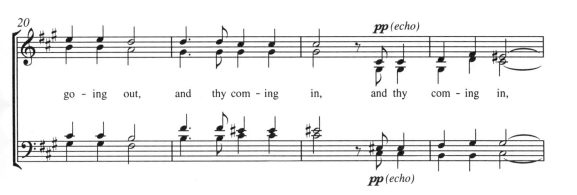

go - ing out,   and thy com - ing   in,   and thy   com - ing in,

from   this   time   forth   for e - ver - more.

IF WE BELIEVE THAT JESUS DIED

Text: 1 Thessalonians 4: 14, 18
Music: John Goss (1800-1880) arr. Harrison Oxley (b.1933)

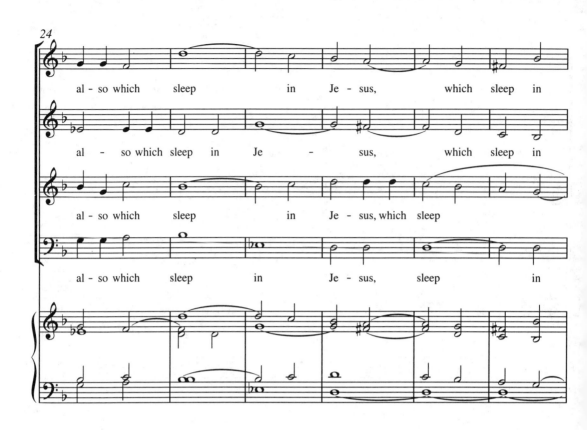

al - so which sleep in Je - sus, which sleep in

al - so which sleep in Je - sus, which sleep in

al - so which sleep in Je - sus, which sleep

al - so which sleep in Je - sus, sleep in

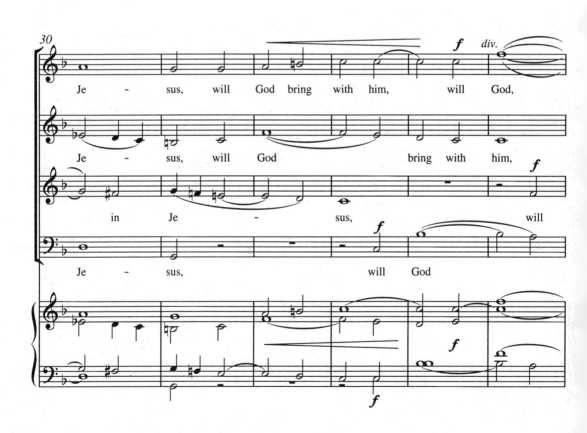

Je - sus, will God bring with him, will God,

Je - sus, will God bring with him,

in Je - sus, will

Je - sus, will God

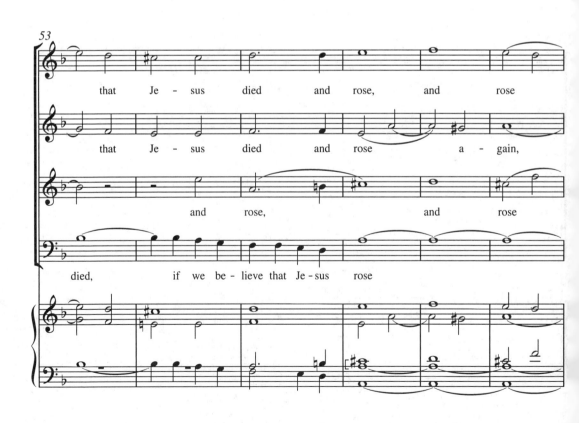

Anthems

IF YE LOVE ME, KEEP MY COMMANDMENTS

Text: John 14:15-17
Music: Thomas Tallis (c.1505-1585)

* 'spirit' should be pronounced 'sprit'

IN THE DARKNESS OF THE GARDEN

Text: Michael Forster (b.1946)
Music: Colin Mawby (b.1936)

1. In the dark - ness of the gar - den, see the tears and bloo - dy
2. In the sor - row of the gar - den, see the friends who fall a -
3. In the si - lence of the gar - den, feel the chill and lead - en

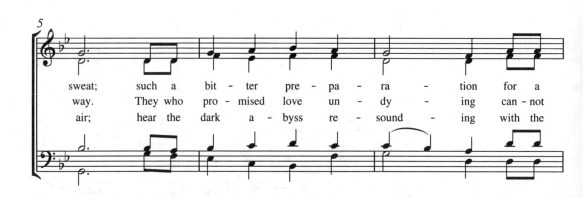

sweat; such a bit - ter pre - pa - ra - tion for a
way. They who pro - mised love un - dy - ing can - not
air; hear the dark a - byss re - sound - ing with the

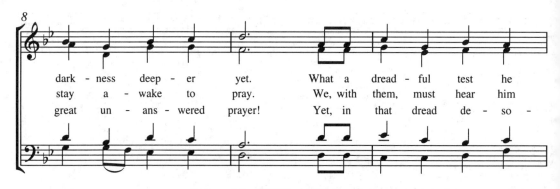

dark - ness deep - er yet. What a dread - ful test he
stay a - wake to pray. We, with them, must hear him
great un - ans - wered prayer! Yet, in that dread de - so -

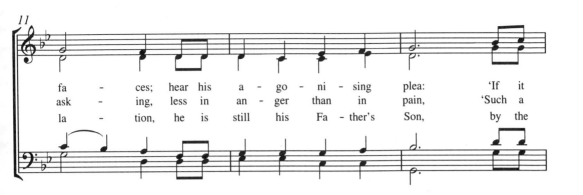

fa - ces; hear his a - go - ni - sing plea: 'If it
ask - ing, less in an - ger than in pain, 'Such a
la - tion, he is still his Fa - ther's Son,

'If it
'Such a
by the

lies with - in your pur - pose, take this cup a - way from me.'
sim - ple task I set you; have you failed me once a - gain?'
Spi - rit's power de - clar - ing, 'Not my will but yours be done.'

IN THE MIDST OF LIFE

Text: from the 'Book of Common Prayer'
Music: Henry Purcell (1659-1695)

This anthem is the second of
'Three Funeral Sentences'.

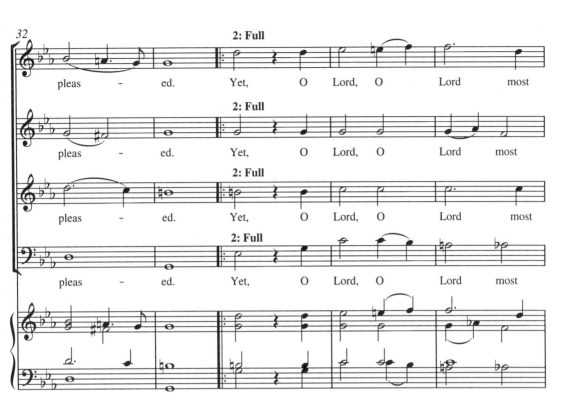

JESU, GRANT ME THIS, I PRAY

Text: 17th century Latin trans. Henry Williams Baker (1821-1877)
Music: Richard Lloyd (b.1933)

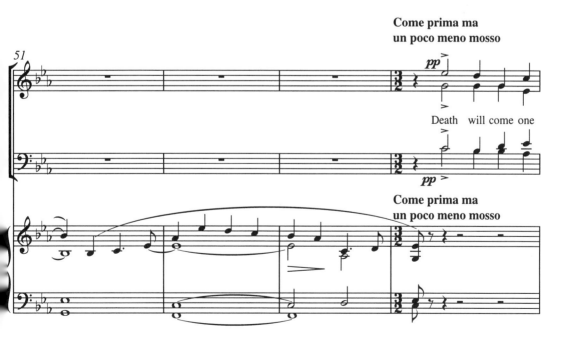

day to me; Je - su, cast me not from thee; dy - ing

(Célestes)

let me still a - bide in thy heart and woun-ded side.

Flute 8' *mp*

Man.

JESU, MY TRUTH, MY WAY

Text: Charles Wesley (1757-1834)
Music: Malcolm Archer (b.1952)

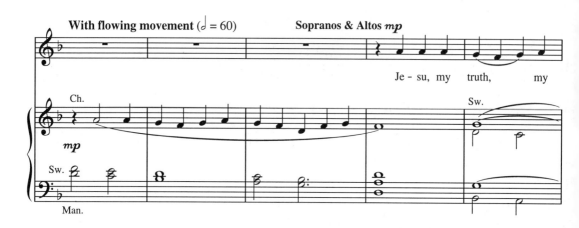

art ... in all things to de-pend on
Man.

de - pend on

thee; O ne - ver, Lord, de - part, but love me,

thee; ne - ver, Lord, de - part,

Ped.

love me to the end.

dim.

JESU, REDEMPTOR OMNIUM

Text: from the Office of Vespers
Music: George Malcolm (1917-1998)

pre — ces tu - i per or - bem ser - vu - li.

3. Memento, rerum conditor,
   nostri quod olim coporis,
   sacrata ab alvo Virginis
   nascendo, formam sumpseris.

4. Testatur hoc praesens dies,
   currens per anni circulum,
   quod solus e sinu Patris
   mundi salus adveneris.

5. Hunc astra, tellus, aequora,
   hunc omne quod caelo subest,
   salutis auctorem novae
   novo salutat cantico.

6. Et nos, beata quos sacri
   rigavit unda sanguinis,
   natalis ob diem tui,
   hymni tributum solvimus.

7. Jesu, tibi sit gloria,
   qui natus es de Virgine,
   cum Patre et almo Spiritu,
   in sempiterna saecula.

Translation (not for performance):

1. Jesu, Redeemer of the world!
   before the earliest dawn of light
   from everlasting ages born,
   immense in glory as in might;

2. Immortal Hope of all mankind!
   in whom the Father's face we see;
   hear thou the prayers thy people pour
   this day throughout the world to thee.

3. Remember, O creator Lord!
   that in the Virgin's sacred womb
   thou wast conceived, and of her flesh
   didst our mortality assume.

4. This ever-blest recurring day
   its witness bears, that all alone,
   from thy own Father's bosom forth,
   to save the world thou camest down.

5. O day! to which the seas and sky,
   and earth and heaven, glad welcome sing;
   O day! which healed our misery,
   and brought on earth salvation's king.

6. We too, O Lord, who have been cleansed
   in thy own fount of blood divine,
   offer the tribute of sweet song,
   on this dear natal day of thine.

7. O Jesu! born of Virgin bright,
   immortal glory be to thee;
   praise to the Father infinite,
   and Holy Ghost eternally.

Anthems

JESUS CHRIST THE APPLE TREE

Text: Anonymous, from the collection of Joshua Smith
Music: Colin Mawby (b.1936),
based on the plainsong 'Vexilla Regis'

* Sopranos or Altos divisi, depending upon the singers available.

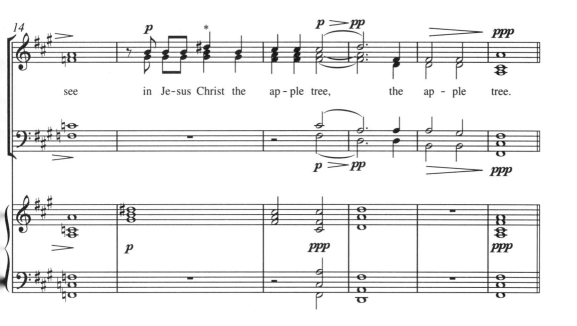

see in Je-sus Christ the ap-ple tree, the ap - ple tree.

Sopranos and Altos

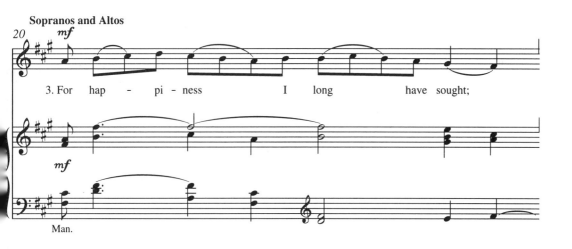

3. For hap - pi - ness I long have sought;

Man.

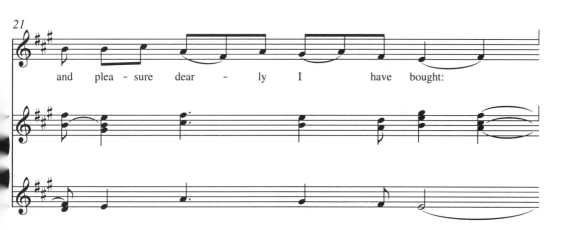

and plea - sure dear - ly I have bought:

* Sopranos or Altos divisi, depending upon the singers available.

241

I missed of all; but now I see

'tis found in Christ the ap - ple tree.

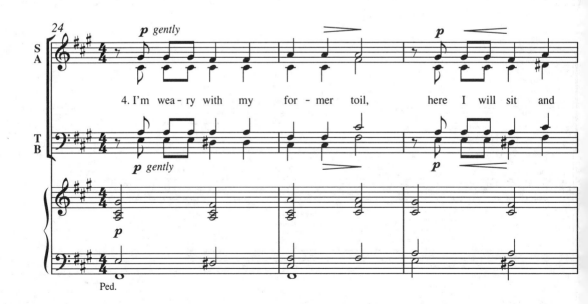

4. I'm wea - ry with my for - mer toil, here I will sit and

With Je-sus Christ the ap - ple tree, with Je-sus Christ the ap - ple tree, the ap - ple tree.

* *Sopranos or Altos divisi, depending upon the singers available.*

JESUS LIVES!

Text: Christian Gellert (1715-1769) trans. Frances Elizabeth Cox (1812-1897)
Music: Colin Hand (b.1929) based on the melody 'St Albinus'
by Henry John Gauntlett (1805-1876)

gloo - my por - tal. Al - le - lu - ia!

Gt. cresc.

Man.   Ped.

Altos (or All except Sopranos) *mf*

Je - sus

dim.

Man.

Sopranos *mf*

Je - sus lives! then, to Je - sus liv - ing,

lives! for us he died; then, a - lone to Je - sus liv - ing,

Altos continue in the absence of sufficient men.

se - ver; life nor death nor pow'rs of hell tear us from this

keep - ing e - ver. Al - le - lu - ia!

Sopranos

All other voices

Je - sus lives! to him the

f

cresc.

Ped.

f

f

f

* Tenors should sing the upper notes.

Anthems

For Neil Collier and Priory Records

JUBILATE DEO

Text: Psalm 100
Music: Malcolm Archer (b.1952)

O be joy-ful in the Lord all ye lands

serve the Lord with glad - ness and

come be-fore his pre - sence with a
song.
Be ye sure
Man.
Be ye
Gt.
Sw.
Ped.
that the Lord he is God.
It is
sure that the Lord he is God.

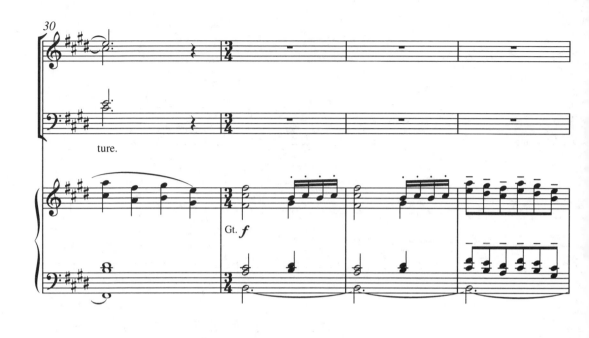

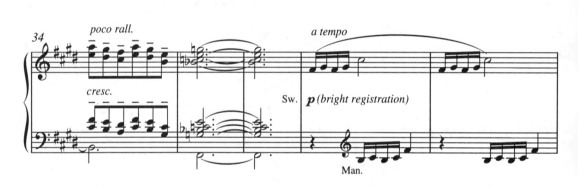

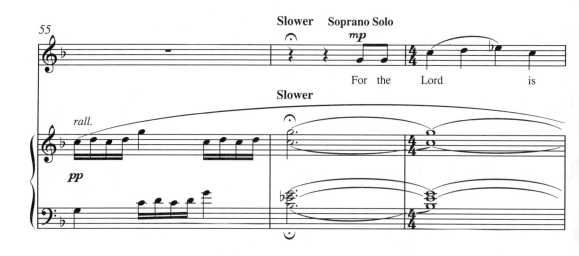

Slower **Soprano Solo**

For the Lord is

Slower

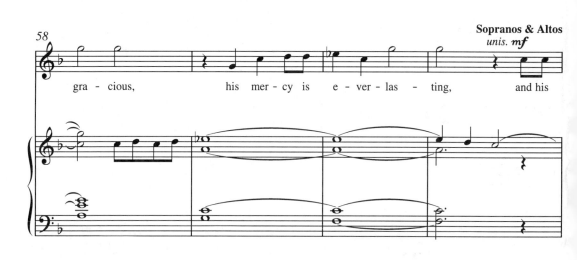

Sopranos & Altos
unis. **mf**

gra - cious, his mer - cy is e - ver - las - ting, and his

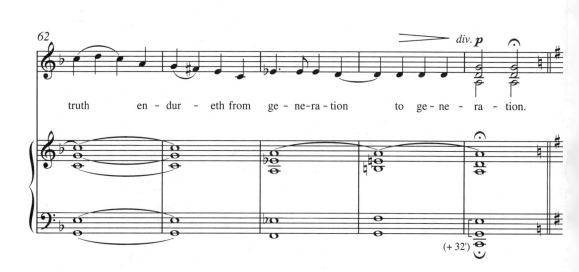

truth en - dur - eth from ge - ne-ra - tion to ge - ne - ra - tion.

(+ 32')

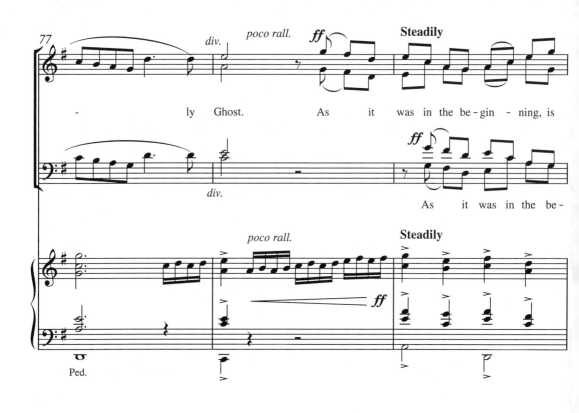

For the choir of Bristol Cathedral, England

JUDGE ETERNAL

Text: Henry Scott Holland
Music: Malcolm Archer (b.1952)

1. Judge e-ter-nal, throned in splen-dour, Lord of lords and King of kings,
2. Still the wea-ry folk are pin-ing for the hour that brings re-lease:

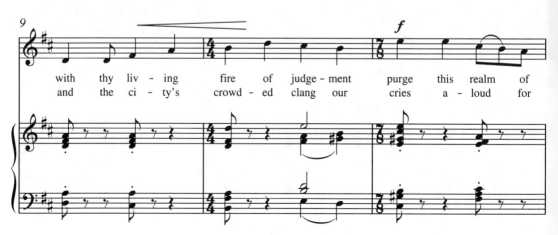

with thy liv-ing fire of judge-ment purge this realm of
and the ci-ty's crowd-ed clang our cries a-loud for

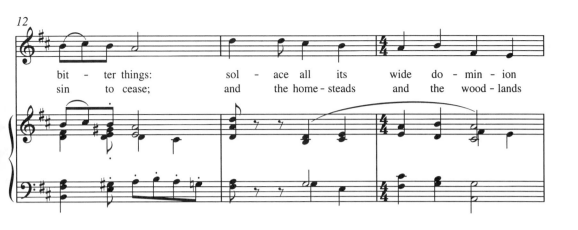

bit - ter things: sol - ace all its wide do - min - ion
sin to cease; and the home - steads and the wood - lands

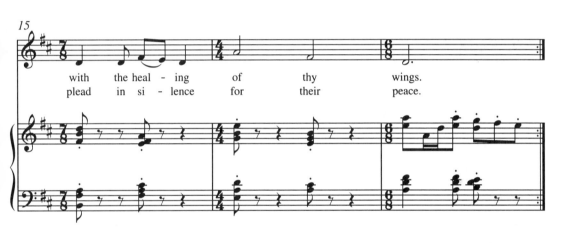

with the heal - ing of thy wings.
plead in si - lence for their peace.

dim.

Ped.

Crown, O God, thine own en-dea-vour, cleave our dark-ness with thy sword:

feed the faint and hun-gry hea-then with the rich-ness of thy word:

cleanse the bo-dy of this em-pire through the glo-ry of the

Anthems

KEEP ME AS THE APPLE OF AN EYE

Text: Psalm 17:8-9
Music: Robert Fielding (b.1956)

Keep me as the ap-ple of an eye, hide
Keep me as the ap-ple of an eye, hide
Keep me as the ap-ple of an eye, hide
Keep me as the ap-ple of an eye, hide

me un-der the sha-dow of thy wings.
me un-der the sha-dow of thy wings.
me un-der the sha-dow of thy wings.
me un-der the sha-dow of thy wings.

LEAD, KINDLY LIGHT

Text: John Henry Newman (1801-1890)
Music: John Stainer (1840-1901)

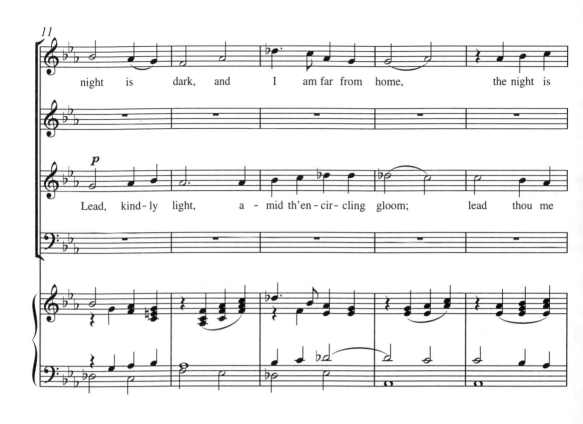

night is dark, and I am far from home, the night is

Lead, kind-ly light, a - mid th'en - cir - cling gloom; lead thou me

dark, and I am far from home. I do not ask to see

Lead, kind-ly light, a -

on, lead thou me on; I do not ask to

Lead, kind-ly light, a -

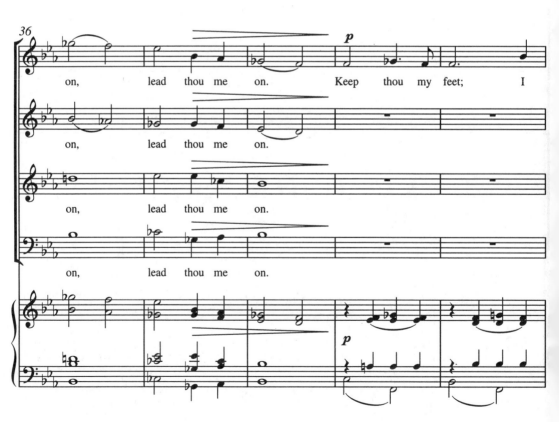

LEAD ME, LORD

Text: Psalm 5:8; 4:9
Music: Samuel Sebastian Wesley (1810-1876)

LET THE PEOPLE PRAISE THEE

Text: Psalm 67
Music: Colin Hand (b.1929)

all the peo - ple praise thee. O let the na - tions re -

joice and be glad, for thou shalt judge the folk

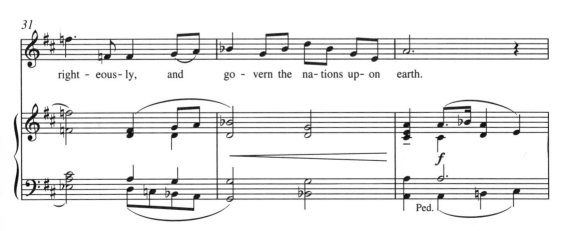

right - eous- ly, and go - vern the na- tions up- on earth.

LIKE AS THE HART

Text: from Psalm 42
Music: Noel Rawsthorne (b.1929)

LO! STAR-LED CHIEFS

Text: Reginald Heber (1783-1826)
Music: William Crotch (1775-1847) from the Oratorio 'Palestine' arr. Colin Hand (b.1929)

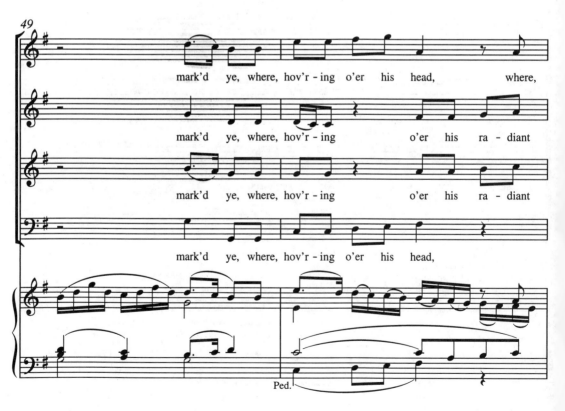

dove's white wings ce-les-tial glo-ry shed, the dove's white wings ce-les-tial

the dove's white wings ce-les-tial glo-ry shed, the dove's white wings ce-les-tial

dove's white wings ce-les-tial glo-ry shed, the dove's white wings ce-les-tial

dove's white wings ce-les-tial glo-ry shed, the dove's white wings ce-les-tial

glo - ry shed?

glo - ry shed?

glo - ry shed?

glo - ry shed?

LORD, HOW GRACIOUS

Text: Psalm 85: 1, 2, 10-13
Music: Harrison Oxley (b.1933)

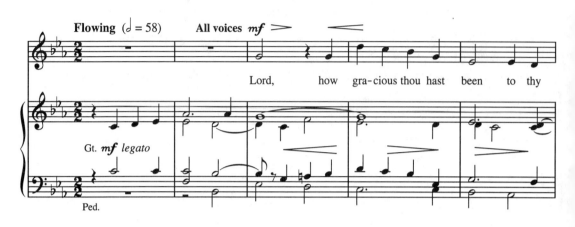

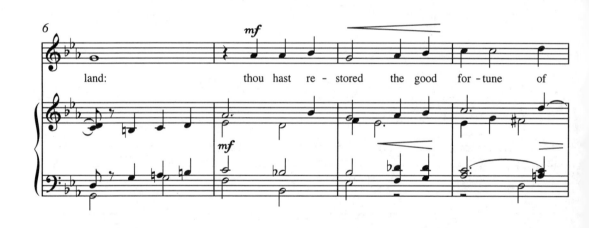

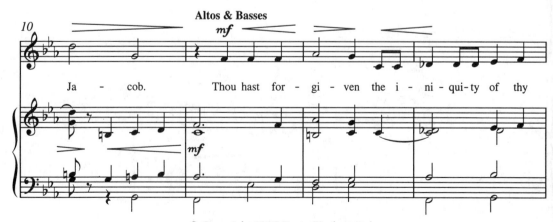

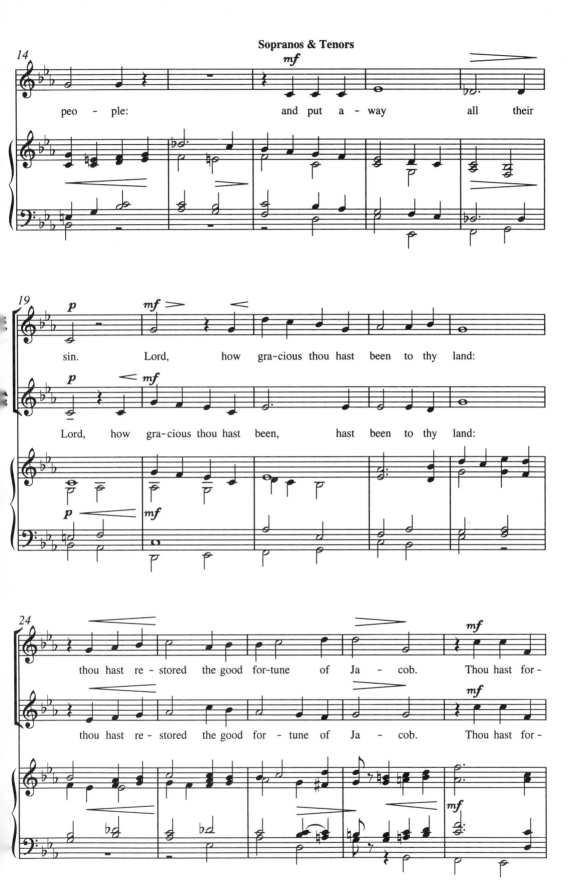

peo - ple: and put a - way   all   their

sin.   Lord,   how gra-cious thou hast   been   to   thy   land:

Lord,   how gra-cious thou hast   been,   hast   been   to   thy   land:

thou hast re - stored   the good for-tune   of   Ja - cob.   Thou hast for -

thou hast re - stored   the good for - tune   of   Ja - cob.   Thou hast for -

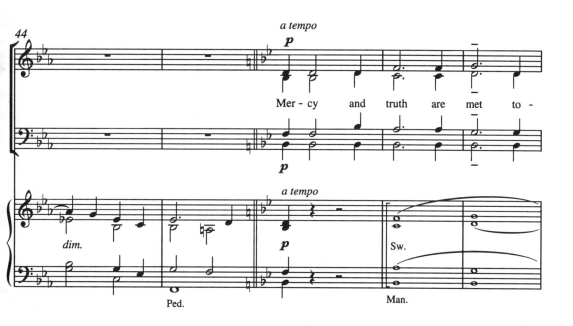

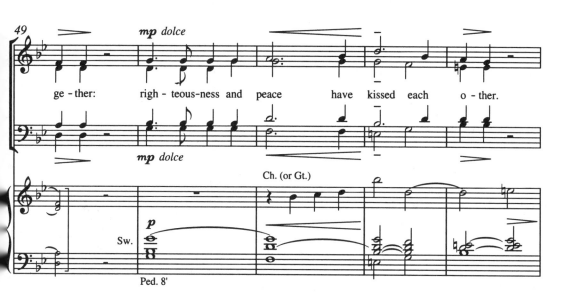

LORD, TEACH US HOW TO PRAY

Text: James Montgomery (1771-1854)
Music: Rodney Bambrick (b.1927)

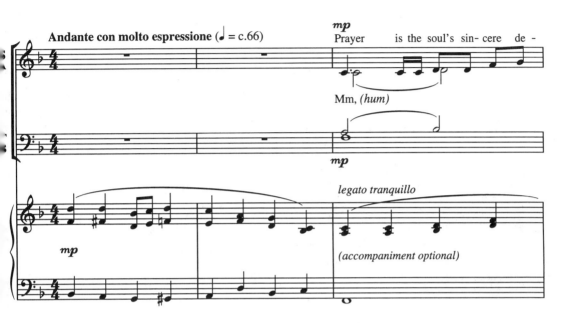

voice re-turn-ing from his ways, while an-gels in their songs re-

while an-gels re-

joice and cry 'be-hold, he prays', 'be-hold, he prays.'

joice

Prayer is the Chris-tian's vi-tal breath, the Chris-tian's na-tive air, our

Ah,

LOVING SHEPHERD OF THY SHEEP
from 'HANSEL AND GRETEL'

Text: based on the hymn by Jane Eliza Leeson (1809-1881)
Music: Engelbert Humperdinck (1854-1921) arr. Harrison Oxley

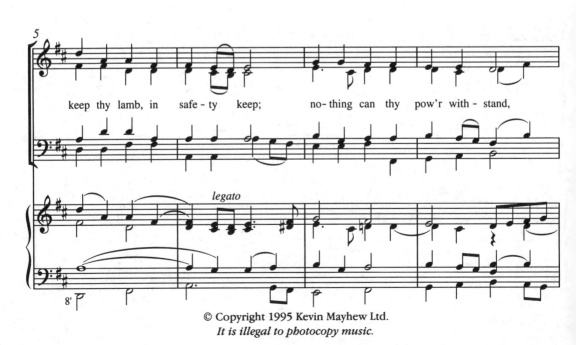

Fa- ther's throne I shall know as I am known.

Fa- ther's throne know as I am known.

till I know as I am known.

till I know as I am known.

espress.

pp

MORNING STAR

Text: J. Scheffler (1657) trans. B. Harvey (1885)
Music: Richard Shephard (b.1949)

Morn- ing star, O cheer-ing sight! Ere thou cam'st how dark earth's might!

Je - sus mine, in me shine, fill my heart with light di - vine.

Morn- ing star, thy glo-ry bright far ex-cels the sun's clear light:

Je - sus be con-stant-ly more than thou-sand suns to me.

*Vowel as in 'but'.

Anthems

For my Father

O ALMIGHTY GOD

Text: from the Scottish Prayer Book
Music: Christopher Tambling (b.1964)

* Divisi Soprano and Bass parts are optional.

haven where they would be, with a grate-ful sense of thy

mer - cies; through Je - sus Christ our Lord. A -

- men.

O CLAP YOUR HANDS

Text: Psalm 47
Music: Malcolm Archer (b.1952)

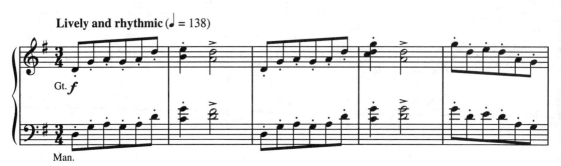

O clap your hands to - ge - ther all ye peo - ple,

shall sub - due the peo - ple un - der us and the

na - tions un - der our feet.

Full Sw. p mf

Ped.

Anthems

O COME, LET US SING UNTO THE LORD

Text: Psalm 95
Music: Christopher Tambling (b.1964)

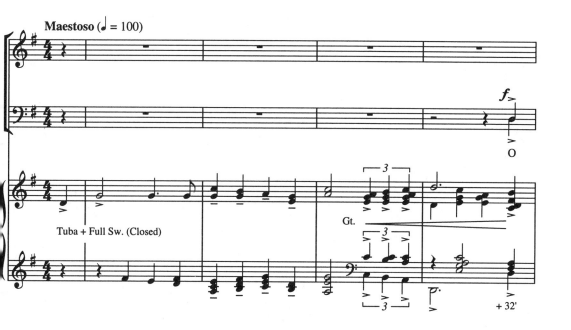

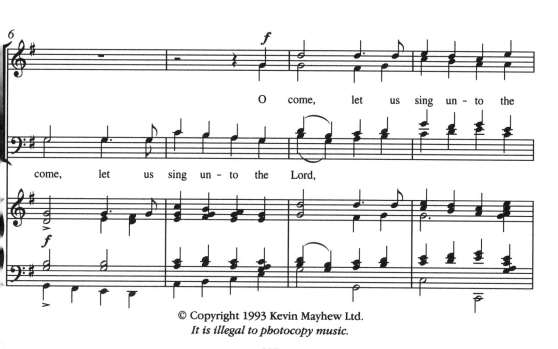

337

him with psalms.

div. mf
For the Lord is a

great God, and a great King a-bove all gods. In his

and a great King a - bove all gods.

hands are all the cor-ners of the earth; and the strength of the hills is

Ped. (32')

kneel be-fore the Lord our ma-ker:

Altos *mf*

kneel be - fore the Lord our ma-ker:

for he is the Lord our

kneel be-fore the Lord our ma-ker:

Tenors & Basses

unis. mf

kneel be - fore the Lord our ma-ker:

mf

Sopranos & Altos

God, and we are the peo-ple of his pas-ture

and the sheep of his

rit.

+ Soft Reed 8'

Sw.

Man.

rit.

now and e - ver shall be. World with - out

World with - out end, A - men.

end, A - men. World with - out end, A - men.

O COME, YE SERVANTS OF THE LORD

Text: Adapted from Psalm 113
Music: Christopher Tye (c.1497-1572)

O FOR A CLOSER WALK WITH GOD

Text: William Cowper (1731-1800)
Music: Charles Villiers Stanford (1852-1924)
based on a melody from the 'Scottish Psalter' (1635) arr. Harrison Oxley (b.1933)

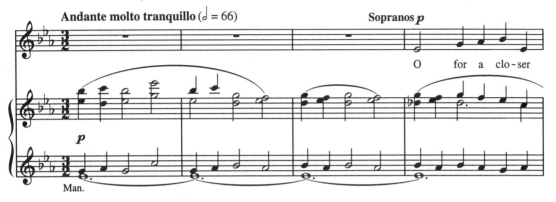

Anthems

O FOR THE WINGS OF A DOVE

Text: Psalm 55:6-7
Music: Felix Mendelssohn (1809-1847) arr. Harrison Oxley (b.1933)

wil - der-ness build me a nest, and re - main there for e - ver at

rest, in the wil - der-ness build me, build me a nest,

and re - main there for e - ver at rest, in the wil - der-ness

build me a nest, and re - main there for e - ver at rest,

O GLADSOME LIGHT

Text: Greek Hymn (before 4th century)
Music: Harrison Oxley (b.1933)

O GOD, OUR HELP IN AGES PAST

Text: Isaac Watts (1647-1748) from Psalm 90
Music: Henry Walford Davies (1869-1941) arr. Harrison Oxley

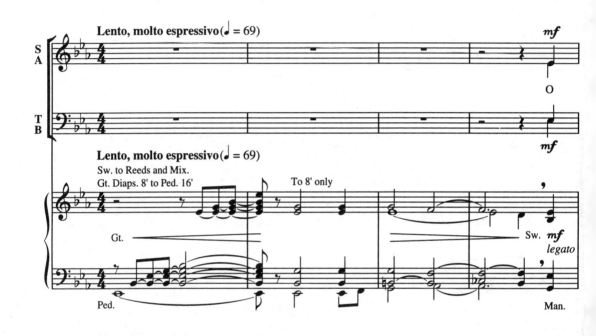

and our de-fence is sure. Be - fore the hills in

or - der stood, or earth re - ceived her frame, from

e - ver - last - ing thou art God, to end - less years the

* _Alternative if notes are found too low:_

O JESUS, I HAVE PROMISED

Text: John Ernest Bode (1816–1874)
Music: Andrew Gant (b.1963)

O LORD, THE MAKER OF ALL THING

Text: from 'The King's Primer' (1545)
Music: William Mundy (c.1529-1591) arr. Harrison Oxley (b.1933)

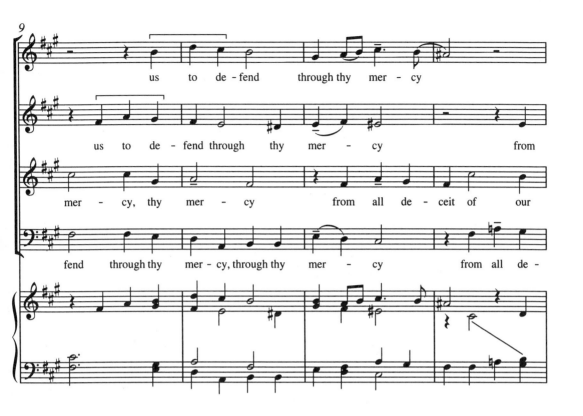

* Optional division of the choir, taking cue size notes at end of phrases.
  Alternatively, sing full throughout.

that we in sin fall not on sleep. O

that we in sin fall not on sleep.

that we in sin fall not on sleep.

that we in sin fall not on sleep.

Fa - ther, through thy bles - sed Son grant us this

O Fa - ther, through thy bles - sed Son grant

O Fa - ther, through thy bles - sed Son

O Fa - ther, through thy bles - sed

O PRAISE GOD IN HIS HOLINESS

Text: Psalm 150
Music: Charles Villiers Stanford (1852-1924)

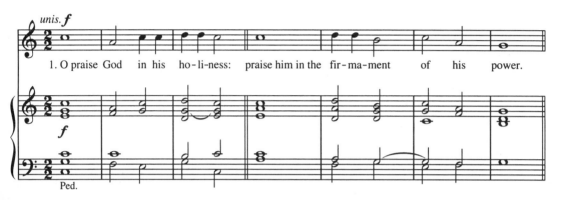

1. O praise God in his ho-li-ness: praise him in the fir-ma-ment of his power.

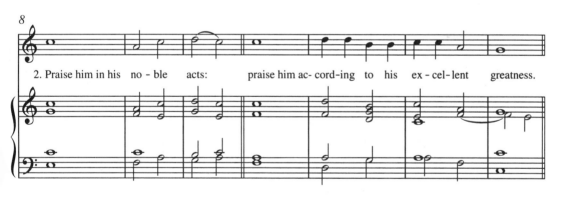

2. Praise him in his no - ble acts: praise him ac- cord-ing to his ex - cel - lent greatness.

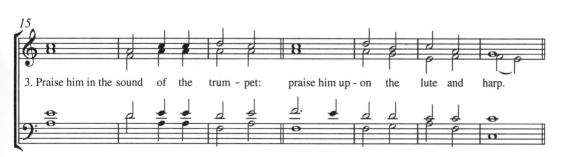

3. Praise him in the sound of the trum - pet: praise him up - on the lute and harp.

4. Praise him in the cym-bals and dan - ces: praise him up-on the strings and pipe.

Tenors & Basses

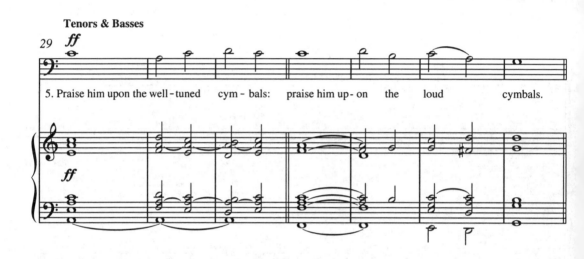

5. Praise him upon the well-tuned cym - bals: praise him up-on the loud cymbals.

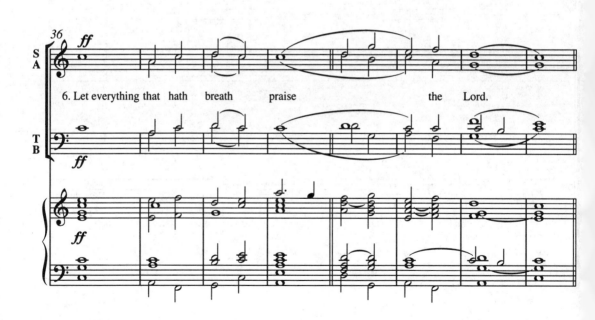

6. Let everything that hath breath praise the Lord.

Glory be to the Father and to the Son: and to the Holy Ghost.

As it was in the beginning, is now and e - ver shall be: world without

end. A - men.

O SACRUM CONVIVIUM

Text: attributed to St Thomas Aquinas (1226-1274)
Music: Malcolm Archer (b.1952)

et fu - tu - rae glo - ri - ae no - bis pig - nus

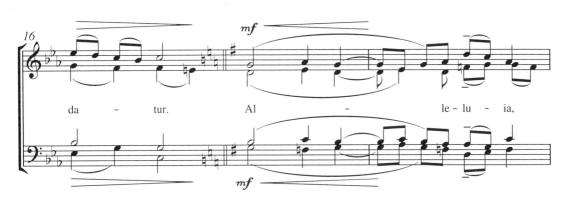

da - tur. Al - le - lu - ia,

al - le - lu - ia, al -

- le - lu - ia, A - men.

O SALUTARIS HOSTIA

Text: Thomas Aquinas (1227-1274)
Music: Malcolm Archer (b.1952)

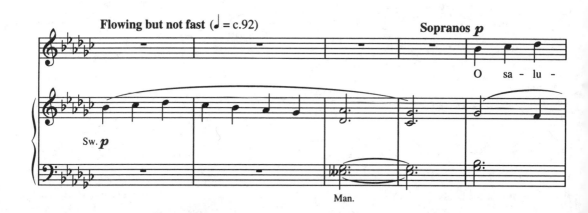

a, qui - a vi - tam si - ne ter - mi - no, no - bis

do - net in pa - tri - a. A - men,

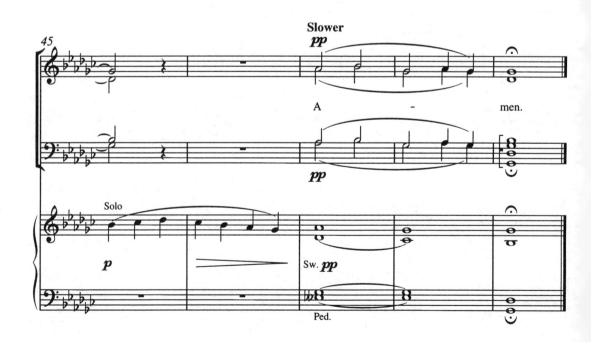

A - men.

Anthems

O SAVIOUR OF THE WORLD

Text: Book of Common Prayer, adapted by Christopher Tambling
Music: Christopher Tambling (b.1964)

O SHOUT TO THE LORD IN TRIUMPH

Text: adapted from Psalm 100
Music: Christopher Tambling (b.1964)

De - o! Glo-ry to the Fa-ther and to the
Son: and to the Ho — ly Spi — rit:
as it was in the be — gin — ning, is now, and

Anthems

O TASTE AND SEE

Text: Psalm 34:8
Music: Ralph Vaughan Williams (1872-1958)

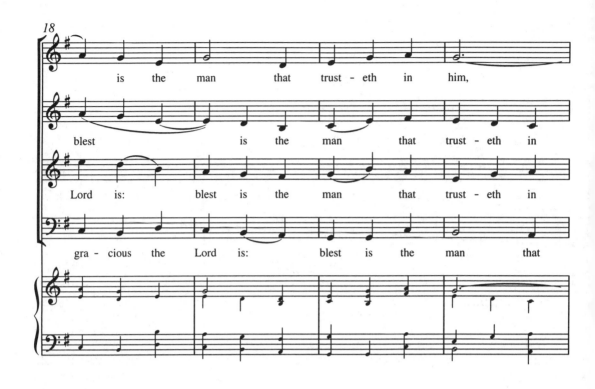

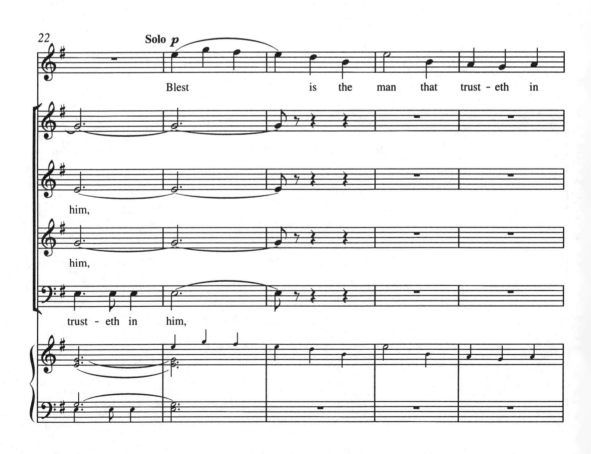

OCULI OMNIUM

Text: Gradual for the Feast of Corpus Christi
Music: Charles Wood (1866-1926)

PEACE, PERFECT PEACE

Text: Bishop E.H. Bickersteth (1825-1906)
Music: Orlando Gibbons (1583-1625)

1. Peace, per-fect peace, in this dark world of sin? The blood of Je-sus whis-pers peace with-in.

2. Peace, per-fect peace, by throng-ing du-ties pressed? To do the will of Je-sus, this is rest.

3. Peace, per-fect peace, with loved ones far a-way? In Je-sus' keep-ing we are safe and they.

4. Peace, per-fect peace, our fu-ture all un-known? Je-sus we know, and he is on the throne.

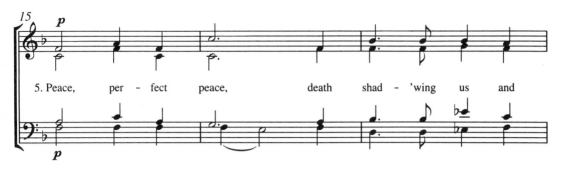

5. Peace, per - fect peace, death shad - 'wing us and

ours? Je - sus has van - quished death and all its pow'rs.

6. It is e - nough: earth's strug - gles soon shall

cease, and Je - sus call us to heav'n's per - fect peace.

PIE JESU from 'REQUIEM'

Text: from the Requiem Mass
Music: Malcolm Archer (b.1952)

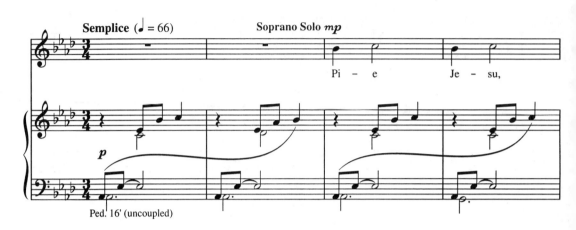

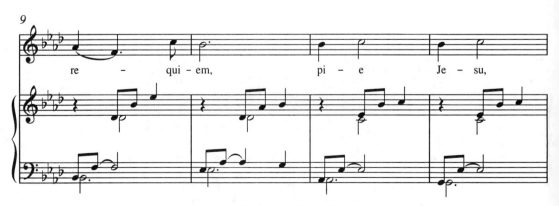

Do - mi - ne, do - na e - is

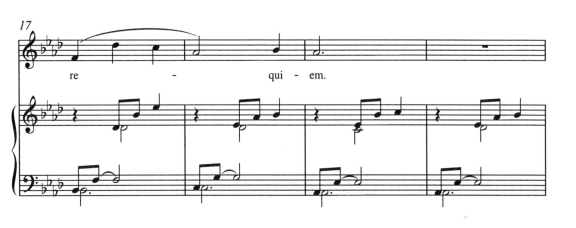

re - qui - em.

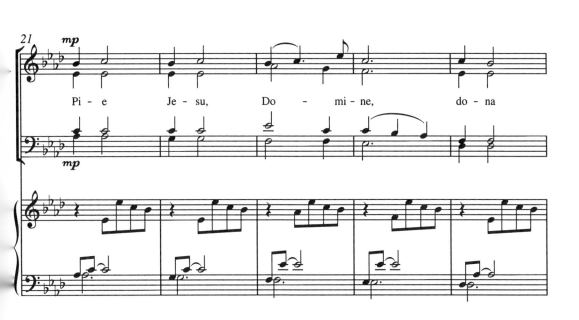

Pi - e Je - su, Do - mi - ne, do - na

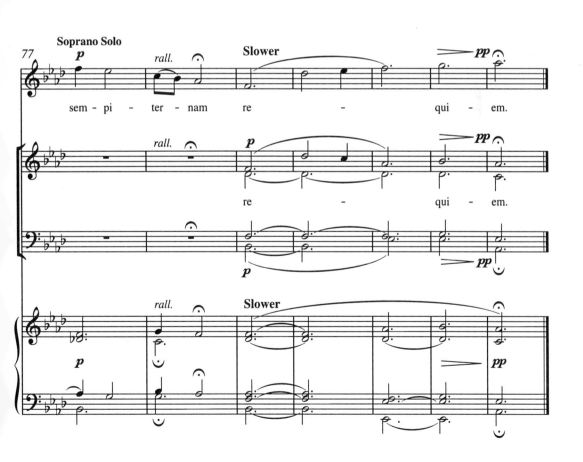

REJOICE IN THE LORD ALWAY

Text: Philippians 4:4-7
Music: Christopher Tambling (b.1964)

* Original words are 'known unto all men'

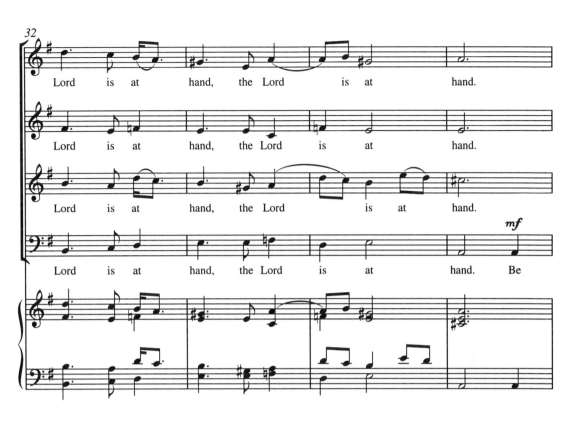

ev - 'ry-thing by prayer, by prayer and sup-pli - ca - tion let your re -

ev - 'ry-thing by prayer, by prayer and sup-pli - ca - tion let your re -

ev - 'ry-thing by prayer, by prayer and sup-pli - ca - tion let your re -

ev - 'ry-thing by prayer, by prayer and sup-pli - ca - tion let your re -

quests be known un - to God. And the peace of God, and the

quests be known un - to God. And the peace of God, and the

quests be known un - to God. And the peace of God, and the

quests be known un - to God. And the peace of God,

REJOICE, THE LORD IS KING

Text: Charles Wesley (1757-1834)
Music: Malcolm Archer (b.1952)

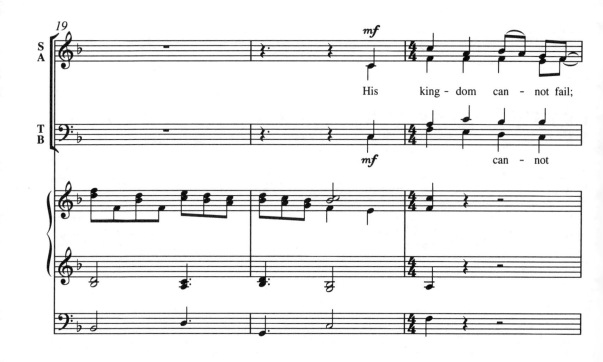

His king - dom can - not fail;

can - not

he rules o'er earth and heav'n; the keys to death and hell

fail; he rules o'er earth and heav'n; the keys to death and

are to our Je - sus giv'n: lift

hell

SOUL OF MY SAVIOUR

Text: 14th century Latin
Music: June Nixon based on the melody 'Anima Christi'
by William Maher (1823-1877)

bathe me in thy tide, wash me with wa - ter

flow - ing from thy side.

S Strength and pro -

A Strength and pro -

T Strength and pro -

B Strength and pro -

For rehearsal only

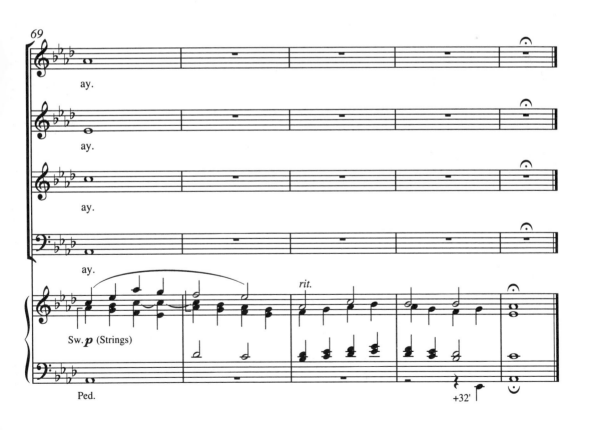

SPIRIT OF GOD

Text: George Croly (1780-1860)
Music: William Lloyd Webber (1916-1982)

445

and make me love thee, and make me love thee as I

make me love thee, make me love thee

make me love thee, make me love thee as I

make me love thee, make me love thee as I

ought to love.

as I ought to love.

ought to love.

ought to love.

88

pas-sion fil-ling all my frame – the bap-ti-sm of the

f animato

93

heav'n des-cen-ded dove, my heart an al-tar, my heart an

mf cresc.

452

SPIRIT OF GOD

Text: Cecil Alexander (1818-1895)
Music: David Terry (b.1975)

keep us thine; nor   leave   the hearts that   once were made fit tem-ples for thy

grace   di - vine;   nor   let us quench thy   sev'n - fold   light;   but

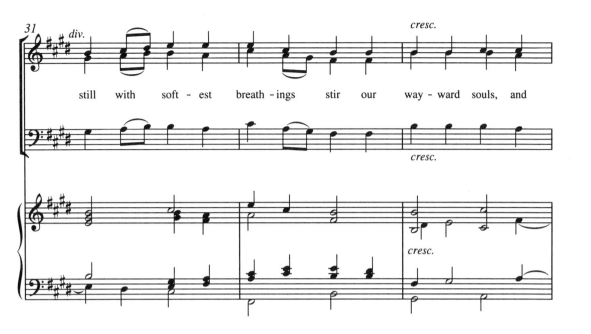

still with soft - est breath -ings stir our way - ward souls, and

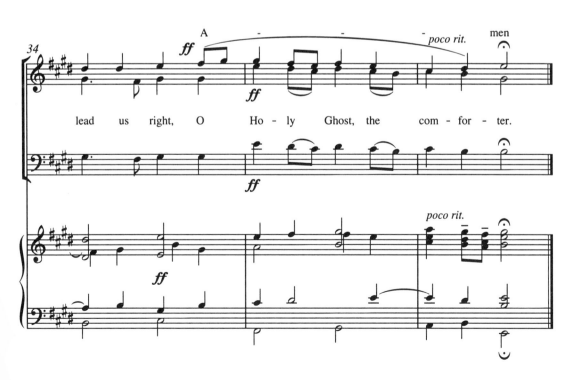

lead us right, O Ho - ly Ghost, the com - for - ter.

TANTUM ERGO

Text: St Thomas Aquinas (1226-1274)
Music: Déodat de Séverac (1873-1921)

THE DAY OF RESURRECTION

Text: St John of Damascus (d. c.754) trans John Mason Neale (1818-1866)
Music: Stanley Vann (b.1910)

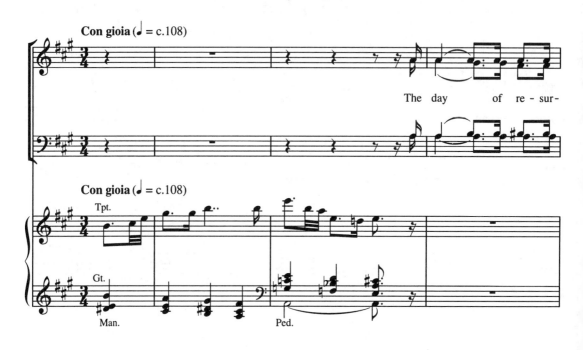

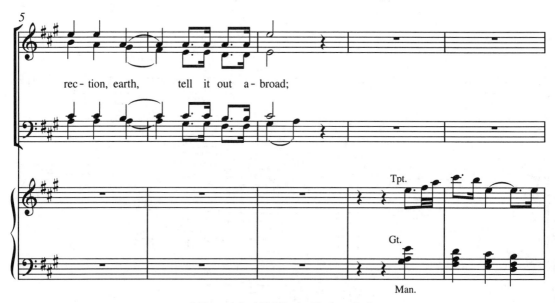

o - ver with hymns, with hymns of vic - to - ry.

Sopranos *mp*

Our

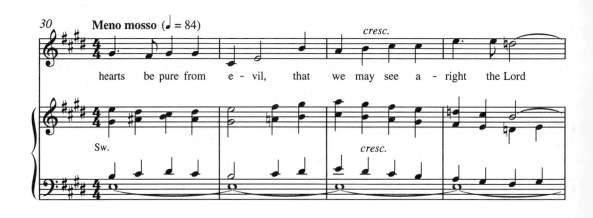

Meno mosso (♩ = 84)

hearts be pure from e - vil, that we may see a - right the Lord

in rays e - ter-nal of re - sur-rec-tion light;

and, list-'ning to his ac-cents, may hear so calm and plain his

own 'All hail', and, hear-ing, may raise the vic - tor strain.

* Hymn tune 'Ellacombe'

THE LORD IS MY SHEPHERD

Text: Psalm 23
Music: Malcolm Archer (b.1952)

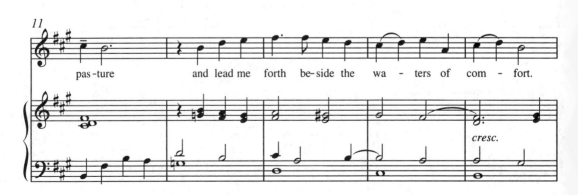

He shall con-vert my soul and bring me forth in the paths of righ-teous-ness for his name's sake.

Un poco animato

Yea, though I walk through the valley of the sha-dow of death, I will fear no

But thy lov-ing kind-ness and mer-cy shall fol-low me

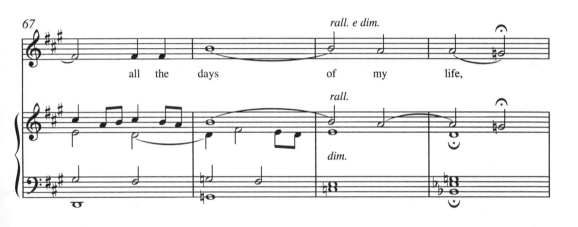

all the days of my life,

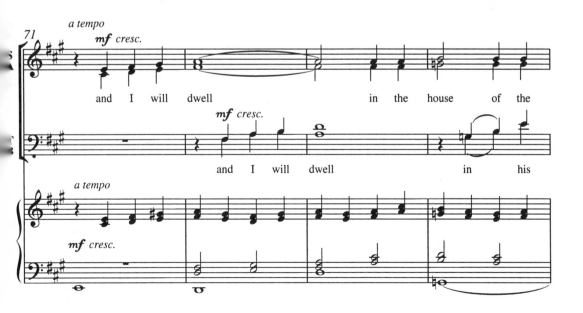

and I will dwell in the house of the

and I will dwell in his

THE LORD IS MY SHEPHERD

Text: Psalm 23
Music: Franz Schubert (1797-1828) arr. John Stainer (1840-1901)

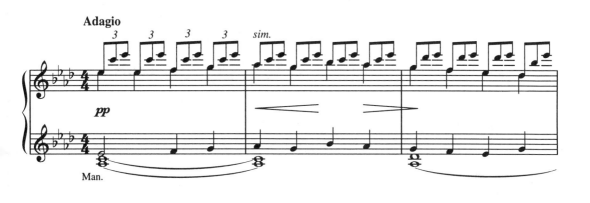

lead – eth me be – side still wa – ters.

lead – eth me be – side still wa – ters.

lead – eth me be – side still wa – ters.

lead – eth me be – side still wa – ters.

He giv – eth peace un- to my

soul: he lead - eth me in paths of good - ness for his, for his name's sake.

THEE WE ADORE

Text: St Thomas Aquinas
Music: Richard Lloyd (b.1933)

pleased to be; both flesh and spi - rit in thy

ment art pleased to be; both flesh and spi - rit in thy

pleased to be; both flesh and spi - rit in thy

pleased to be; both flesh and spi - rit in thy

pre - sence fail, yet here thy pre - sence we de - vout - ly

hail.

unis. **pp** *ben sostenuto*

O blest Me -

unis. **pp** *ben sostenuto*

pp

thee. And thou, O Christ, for e - ver pre-cious be.

thee. And thou, O Christ, for e - ver pre - cious be.

thee. And thou, O Christ, for e - ver pre-cious be.

thee. And thou, O Christ, for e - ver pre-cious be.

mp

poco a poco cresc. e accel.

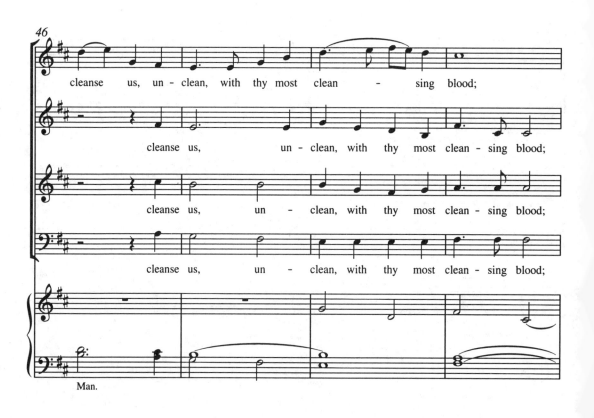

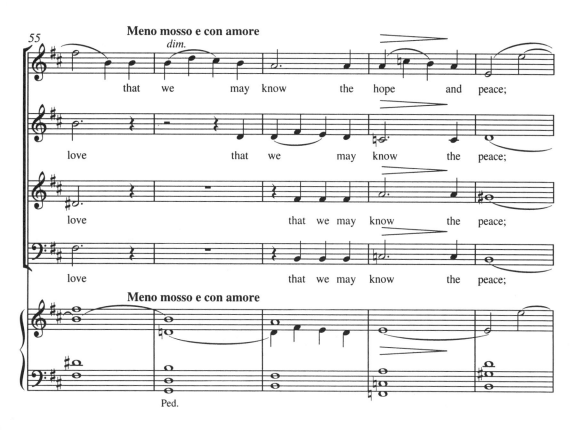

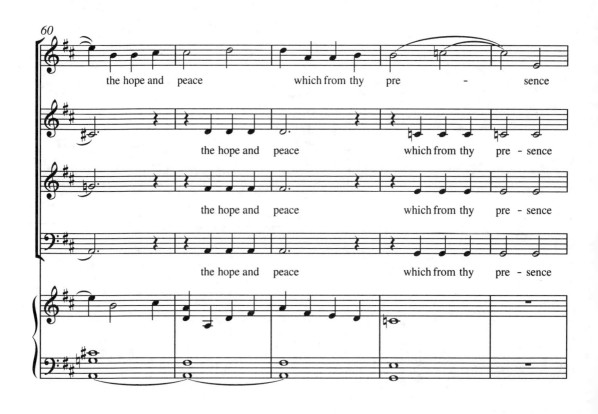

the hope and peace which from thy pre - sence

the hope and peace which from thy pre - sence

the hope and peace which from thy pre - sence

the hope and peace which from thy pre - sence

flow.

flow.

flow.

flow.

pp

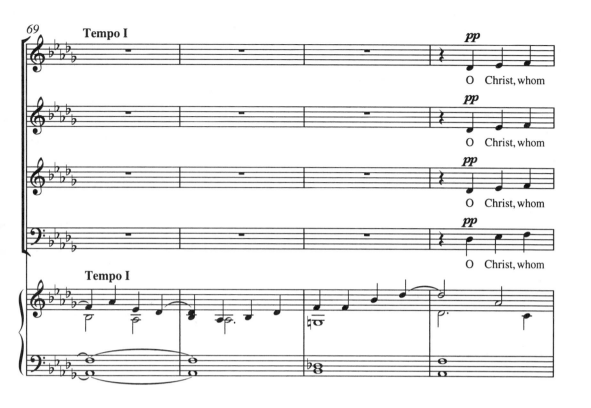

thirst for soon our por - tion be, to gaze on

what we thirst for soon our por - tion be, to gaze on

thirst for soon our por - tion be, to gaze on

thirst for soon our por - tion be, to gaze on

thee un-veil'd and see thy face, the vis - ion, the vis - ion, the

thee un-veil'd and see thy face, the vis - ion, the vis - ion, the

thee un-veil'd and see thy face, the vis - ion, the vis - ion, the

thee un-veil'd and see thy face, the vis - ion, the vis - ion, the

Man.

THERE SHALL A STAR APPEAR from 'CHRISTUS'

Text: Numbers 24:17; Psalm 2:9
Chorale text and melody: Philipp Nicolai (1556-1608)
Music: Felix Mendelssohn (1809-1847)
English Text and Organ arrangement by Harrison Oxley (b.1933)

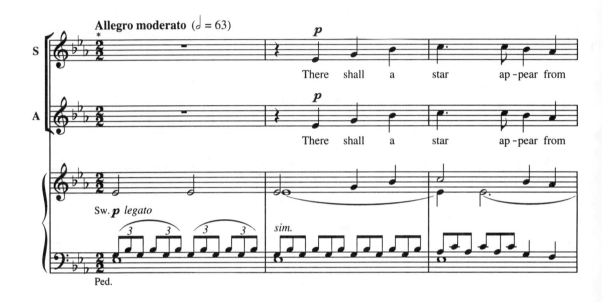

* Originally in $\frac{4}{4}$

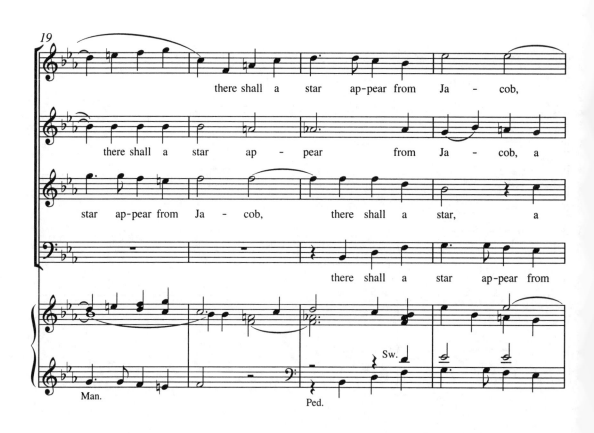

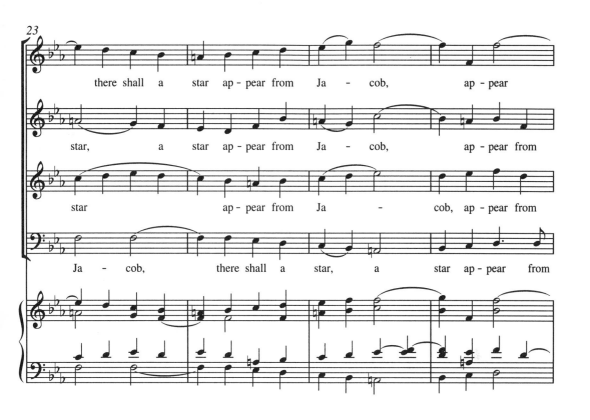

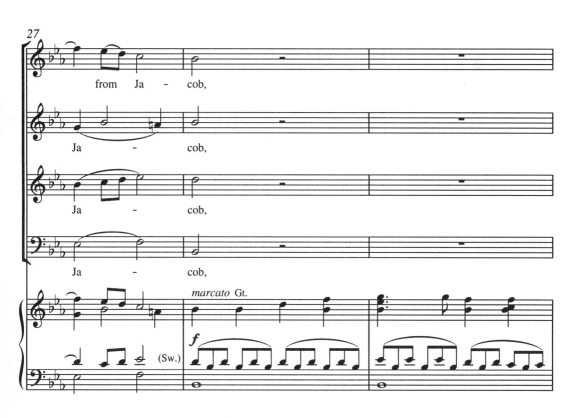

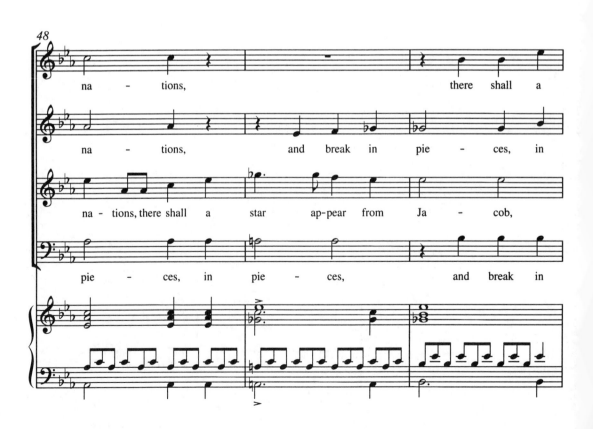

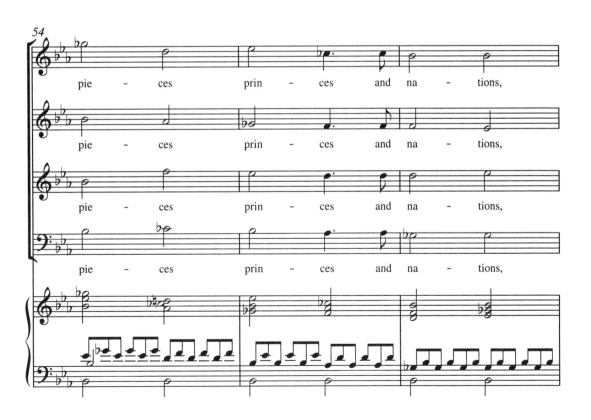

and break in pie - ces prin - ces and

and break in pie - ces prin - ces and

and break in pie - ces prin - ces and

and break in pie - ces prin - ces and

na - tions, there shall a

na - tions,

na - tions, there shall a star ap -

na - tions, there

la - tion. Shine bright, world's light, ra - diance dart - ing, truth im - part - ing,

THOU GOD OF TRUTH AND LOVE

Text: Charles Wesley (1757-1834)
Music: Malcolm Archer (b.1952)

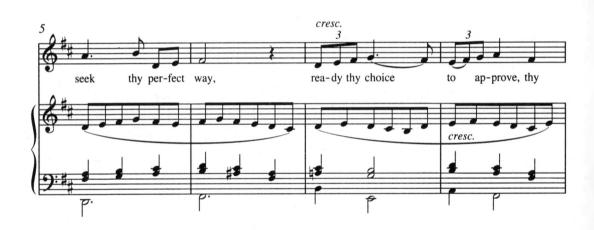

THOU WILT KEEP HIM IN PERFECT PEACE

Text: from Scripture
Music: Samuel Sebastian Wesley (1810-1876)

9 (Basses)
poco accel.

dark - ness is no dark - ness with thee, but the

poco accel.

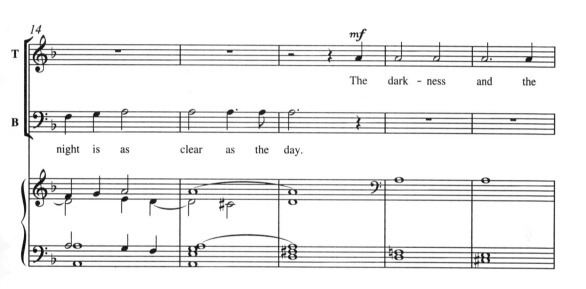

14

T

The dark - ness and the

B

night is as clear as the day.

mf

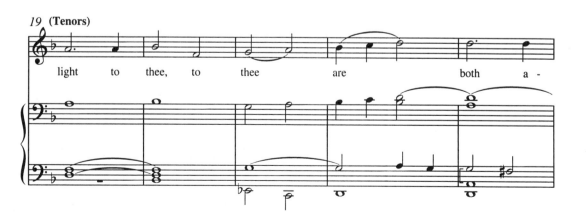

19 (Tenors)

light to thee, to thee are both a -

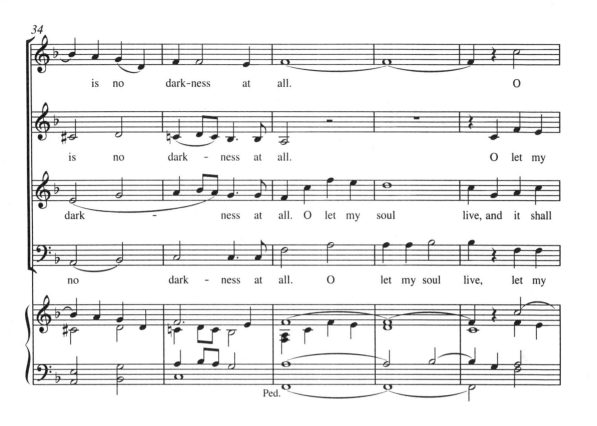

34

is no dark-ness at all. O

is no dark - ness at all. O let my

dark - ness at all. O let my soul live, and it shall

no dark - ness at all. O let my soul live, let my

Ped.

39 *cresc.* *poco accel.*

let my soul live, and it shall praise thee.

cresc. *mf*

soul live, it shall praise thee, for thine, thine is the

cresc. *mf*

praise thee, and it shall praise thee, for thine is the

cresc. *mf*

soul live, and it shall praise thee, for thine is the

poco accel.

cresc. *mf*

Man.

THY CLEAR LIGHT

Text: John Hunter (1848-1917)
Music: Traditional Irish melody arr. Rodney Bambrick (b.1927)

do in my poor days are al – ways two, help me, op-

pressed by things un – done, O thou whose deeds and dreams were

one.

Largamente

Sopranos & Altos *mf*

Though what I dream and what I do in my poor

TO GOD ALL PRAISE AND GLORY

Text: J.J. Schütz trans. Frances Elizabeth Cox (1812-1897)
Music: Alan Viner (b.1951)

through all grief dis - tres - sing, an e - ver - pre - sent help and stay, our

joy and peace and bles - sing. As with a mo - ther's

ten - der hand he leads his own, his chos - en band: to God all praise and

glo - ry.

Thus all my glad-some way a-long I sing a-loud thy

prai - ses, that all may hear the grate-ful song my voice un-wear-ied

rai - ses. Be joy-ful in the Lord, my heart; both

soul and bo-dy bear your part: to God all praise, to

God all praise and glo - ry.

TRIUNE GOD, IN LOVE RESPLENDENT

Text: Michael Forster (b.1946)
Music: Christopher Tambling (b.1964)

greater story, never fully to be told!

Tenors & Basses *unis.*

Holy Spirit, rest upon us that the many may be

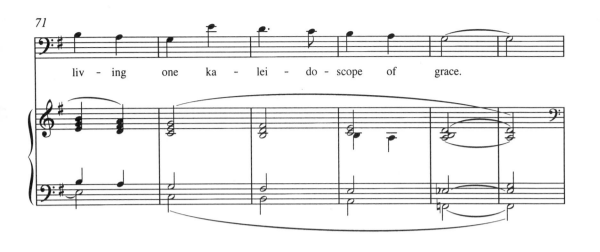

liv - ing one ka - lei - do - scope of grace.

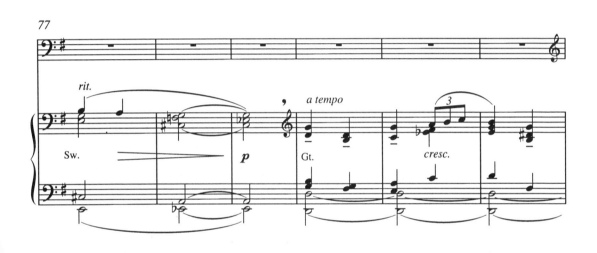

For Andrew Carwood

VENI, SANCTE SPIRITUS

Text: The Order of Mass for Pentecost Sunday
Music: Andrew Moore (b.1954)

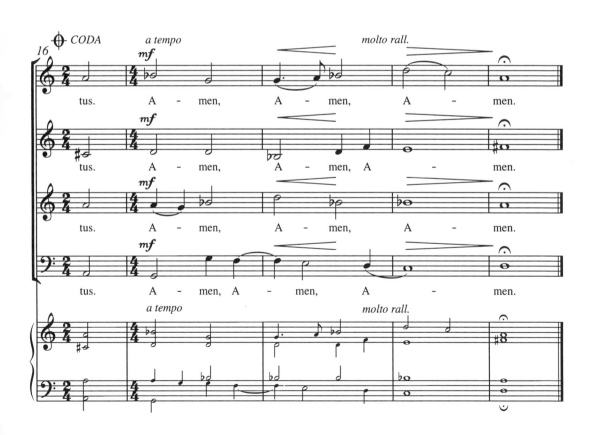

VERITAS MEA

Text: Psalm 89:24

Music: George Malcolm (1917-1998)

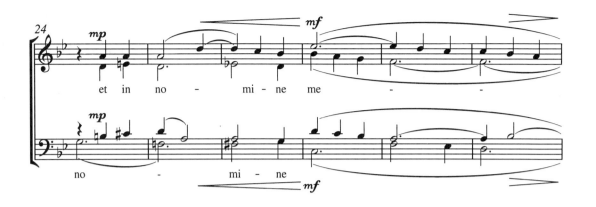

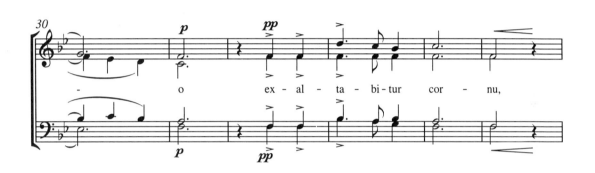

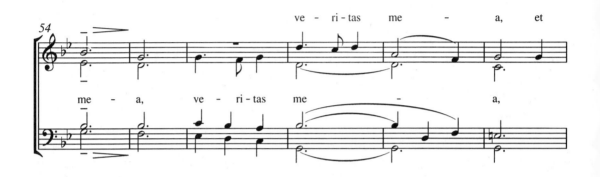

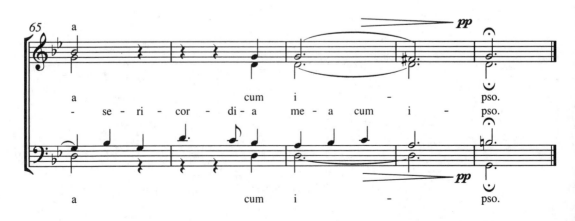

WHEN I SURVEY THE WONDROUS CROSS

Text: Isaac Watts (1674-1748)
Music: Christopher Tambling (b.1964)

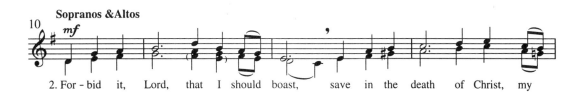

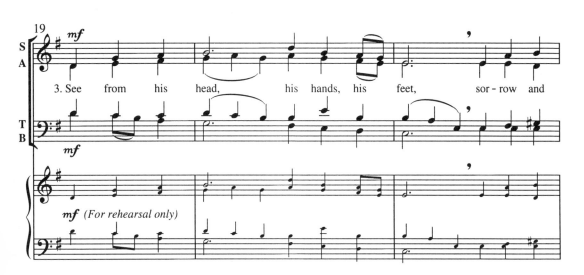

love flow min - gled down; did e'er such love and sor - row meet, or thorns com - pose so rich a crown?

Tenors & Basses

4. His dy - ing crim - son like a robe, spreads o'er his bo - dy on the

tree; then I am dead to all the globe, and all the globe is dead to me.

5. Were the whole realm of na-ture mine, that were a pre - sent far too small; love so a - maz - ing, so di - vine, de - mands my soul, my life, my all.

WHEN MORNING GILDS THE SKIES

Text: 19th century, trans. Edward Caswall (1814-1878)
Music: Philip Marshall (b.1921)

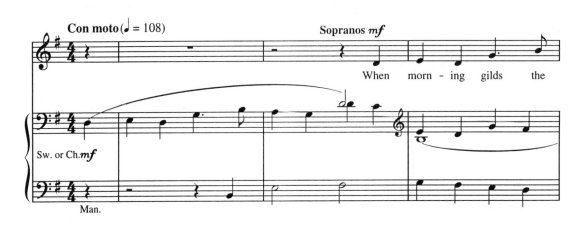

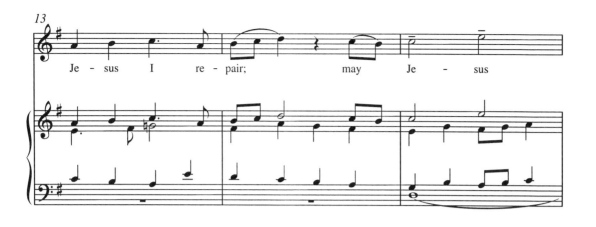

WHILE CHRIST LAY DEAD

Text: Christina Georgina Rossetti (1830-1894)
Music: Stanley Vann (b.1910)

hope un - done:

Solo

Man.

poco accel.

cresc.

Ped.

Poco più mosso

f

till, when bright Eas - ter dews im - pearled the chil - ly bu - rial

f

f

YE CHOIRS OF NEW JERUSALEM

Text: St Fulbert of Chartres (c.1028) trans. Robert Campbell (1814-1868) and others
Music: Charles Villiers Stanford (1852-1924)

joy. For Ju - dah's Li - on bursts his

chains, crush-ing the ser-pent's head; and cries a-loud,

fore. Tri - um - phant in his glo - ry

fore. Tri - um - phant in his glo - ry

fore. Tri - um - phant in his glo - ry

fore. Tri - um - phant in his glo - ry

now to him all pow'r is giv'n;

now to him all pow'r is giv'n;

now to him all pow'r is giv'n;

now to him all pow'r is giv'n;